George Gissing: Critical Essays

GEORGE GISSING: CRITICAL ESSAYS

edited by
Jean-Pierre Michaux

VISION
and
BARNES & NOBLE

Vision Press Limited
11-14 Stanhope Mews West
London SW7 5RD

and

Barnes & Noble Books
81 Adams Drive
Totowa, NJ 07512

ISBN (UK) 0 85478 404 7
ISBN (US) 0 389 20061 1

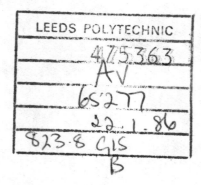
Printed by St. Edmundsbury Press,
Bury St. Edmunds, Suffolk.
Typeset by Chromoset Ltd.
Shepperton, Middlesex.
Bound by Mansell Bookbinders Ltd.
Witham, Essex.
MCMLXXXI

Contents

Foreword

In collecting this series of essays and articles on George Gissing we have attempted to try and present the reader with a selection of wide-ranging essays dealing with Gissing the man as well as Gissing the writer. Though we may speak of a "Gissing revival" (a phrase widely used by critics for the last twenty years) there have been few critical anthologies about the Victorian novelist.

George Gissing wrote at a period when important changes were well on the way: a change of ethics with the emergence of the New Woman, a social awakening in politics which accompanied the rapid evolution of the industrial world, a turning-point in the literary scene with the evolving status of novelists. To all these essential facts we must add and take into account the keen sensibility of an alienated writer who led a life of hardship, and who went through a number of woeful experiences so as to go on writing novels of his time, for Gissing belongs undoubtedly to the Victorian era.

With Q.D. Leavis we cannot but agree when she speaks of his "one permanent contribution to the English novel".[1] Gissing's standing among the major Victorian novelists has been growing steadily over the past decade.

This collection of essays will provide a wide basis for reappraisal of the writer and his works. It comprises two parts. Part One deals essentially with Gissing the man, his unusual temperament, the intellectual outcast he considered himself to be, how he tackled vital contemporary issues and attempted to provide an answer in his own domain. Part Two consists of critical articles focusing on essential aspects of his best known novels in terms of style, theme, structure, sociology, as well as other essays shedding light on less important factors which are nevertheless crucial for a fair understanding of Gissing's works.

We are made to reconsider the importance of his contribution to the literary edifice and his achievement as a truly Victorian novelist.

In this anthology we have attempted to bring together as many different viewpoints and perspectives as possible so as to give the student of Gissing an idea of the wide range in the critical response to his novels.

We shall be happy if we have but added a stone to Gissing's cairn by making important essays available, some of which are difficult to find since they are scattered in a number of publications.

J.P.M.

1 Q.D. Leavis, "Gissing and the English Novel", *Scrutiny*, VII, June 1938, pp. 75-6.

Acknowledgements

I wish to acknowledge the kind help of Professor Coustillas whose invaluable advice and experience on the subject have made this book possible.

Preparation of this anthology has been expedited by the secretarial help of Mme. Yveline Michaux.

All possible care has been taken to trace ownership of the selections included and to make full acknowledgement for their use.

PART ONE
General Studies

1

George Gissing, A Character Sketch

by ELLEN GISSING*

A character that has many sides is always a puzzle to the casual observer, for in it there appear to be more than the usual contradictions. Yet, in spite of the conflict of motives, which exists in most of us, there is generally, if there is anything at all of worth, some guiding principle which, when grasped, gives a clue to the whole, and acts as a key to many doors hitherto closed.

In the case of George Gissing these remarks are particularly true. There can hardly be any writer of whom such contradictory statements have been made—statements which, none the less, often contain, for those who knew him well, a great degree of truth. It is when one side of a character is made to take the place of the whole, and is enlarged upon without a modifying touch from the actual facts which show it in a wholly different light, that the untrue portrait takes the place of the true, and we turn aside saying, "This is not a picture of the man we know".

It may be of interest to give a brief sketch of this complex character, as he appeared to those who knew him well—perhaps as well as he knew himself. Let us consider for a moment the effect produced on a boy of ability much beyond the average— on one who had gained every possible distinction from his earliest school-days, and was conscious that his outlook was

* "George Gissing, A Character Sketch" by Ellen Gissing: reprinted from *Nineteenth Century*, C II, September 1927, pp. 417-24.

quite different from that of his school-fellows—by the sudden withdrawal of his one and only steadying force. At this period of his life he had one lode-star, and that was his father. To him he looked for guidance in all matters; for not only had he a deep devotion to him, but also he felt that his father was the only person who really understood him, whose words, therefore, were worth listening to, and the only person whose learning was such that he could trust him for guidance along the path which even at that early age allured him—the path of knowledge. His one desire was to pursue all kinds of learning, up to the point which he felt few ever reached. For he found that none of the boys of his own age, and very few people of riper years, with whom he came into contact, ever experienced that burning of the heart for knowledge which he possessed. In his father alone he found a companion to his taste, but this sole companion died when Gissing was but thirteen; and in losing him he lost what was, as far as his intellectual life was concerned, his whole world. Let us picture a boy of thirteen, strongly conscious of powers of brain, and filled with the love of knowledge, with no chance of a companion with whom to share his interests; then let us consider if such circumstances could not foster a certain degree of proud isolation, though quite involuntary—an isolation thrust upon him by the fact that those of his own age were utterly unable to enter into his mind. In saying this we must remember that his brothers were both some years younger than himself; it was therefore natural that the sympathy which they were able to give him later was, as yet, impossible.

In our consideration of his mental capacity we must remember that in his younger days he possessed great physical strength, sufficient to enable him to endure enormous hardships, as was proved later. For his physical well-being a great amount of exercise, much fresh air, and games of all kinds were imperative; but from these he always completely withdrew himself. All such things he looked upon as a waste of time. Although he delighted in long rambles in the country, all his time was needed for study, and in his early days he was usually so placed that the unspoiled country was quite beyond his reach. Some amusing caricatures drawn by him when a boy are still preserved. In them both himself and his brothers are represented; and beneath that which bears his name are the significant words, "Vote for no walks". Thus we behold the development of his mental powers taking place in utter disregard of the body, through which alone they were enabled to perform their work to full advantage. Side by side with his mental capacity must be considered his love of home life and the affection which he bore towards his own family, whose sympathy and understanding he was most anxious to gain at all times—traits unusually developed in one of his age. These points are brought out very clearly in his early letters written shortly after the death of his father.

As a boy he was tall and strong, though pale with close study; his preoccupied air was not attractive to other boys, nor was his determined and somewhat dogmatic way of making statements on different topics: "A mere prig", many would say. Indeed, some writers today speak of "priggishness" as being one of his objectionable qualities, but they do not know the whole man. His knowledge was no mere affectation, and his desire to instruct others was free from all thought of self: let it but be necessary to help some fumbler in learning, though it were but one step on the way, and all else was forgotten in the wish to be of use. No pains were spared, no patience was too great, so long as the glance of intelligence in the eye of the listener showed that his words had been understood.

This was the boy who passed on to a boarding-school, after his father's death, feeling, we cannot doubt, quite alone as far as intellectual companionship was concerned, and shutting himself up in his spare time to do extra reading, or to master some subject that interested him. This was the boy who, later, at the age of seventeen, passed on to Owens College, Manchester, with a heart beating high with hopes of future distinction, and with a still deeper hope of satisfying that thirst for knowledge which had, from the first, possessed him. It is easy to see, as the daily grind went on—incessant overwork, to the complete exclusion both of exercise and of refreshment for the body or relaxation for the mind—that the one and only thing longed for—a little human sympathy which would provide an outlet for his over-taxed mind—might quite easily be sought in the wrong direction, and intimacies formed which would prove disastrous. This was indeed the case, and, on account of the further disgrace into which he fell through financial difficulties, his brilliant achievements at college came to nothing. He left under a dark cloud, and determined that his fresh life should begin far away from his own home, in the continent of America.

Though, at this juncture, Gissing's own people were near him, and might have been of some avail, we can well imagine that from them he could no longer gain solace. Was it not he who had hoped to be their guide and their helper in all matters? And now all such hopes were dashed to the ground. Remembering the characteristics we have already noticed in the boy, we still realise that the isolation which had resulted from Gissing's overwhelming love of learning was trifling compared with that caused by the present feeling of disgrace. Moreover, as his quick return from America showed, he was determined to hold to an ill-assorted friendship which he had made at Manchester, and in marrying one with whom any real companionship was impossible he showed that side of his nature which was especially strong—constancy of affection and faithfulness to those who had a right to look to him for help. Some writers on Gissing have lamented the "amorous propensities" which led him into so much disaster. True, it was only in his last marriage that he found the companionship he so much needed, but to speak of "amorous propensities" hardly expresses one of Gissing's most strongly marked characteristics—his desire for a home of his own, and for the kind of domestic life which he had seen about him when a boy, and which, to him, was an ideal. Moreover, a fierce Socialism was strong within him in these early years; he was certain that an equal amount of good might be got out of any class, if each were but rightly treated; and indeed, through the help of those of his relations who were determined to bring him assistance, much was accomplished in this direction, and there seemed at first some hope even for that early marriage. The story has yet to be told, however, of the domestic miseries through which he passed, and of the number of times that his wife was received back and helped to begin yet again. And to the burden of those years of unspeakable struggle and domestic misery was added the dire need of money. His novels *Workers in the Dawn* and *The Unclassed* emerged from this period. Amid, these almost insuperable difficulties, one determination of Gissing's stood firm—he never appealed to his own home for money, nor allowed his mother to know of the extreme privations through which he was passing. In no circumstances would he draw upon her small resources, some of which he knew would be at his disposal if all the truth were revealed to her. When we read in account of this writer of "his unhappy, uncomfortable and often embittered egoism", we feel that the words are true; for, by his own folly, he had brought upon himself exactly the circumstances which caused such "embittered egoism", and which frustrated every hope with which his life had begun. Where was the quiet life of the scholar and the thinker? Where was that peace and order so necessary for any good creative work? Yet to cease to be a scholar, or to cease to write fiction, was impossible for him. His domestic difficulties put an end to all friendly intercourse with others, and he was thrown entirely upon himself—the worst thing that could happen to a character already too self-centred owing to the fact that he saw more deeply into life than his fellow-men. This kind of egoism might well have become an "embittered egoism", for in looking back, though still hardly more than a boy, he felt that the hope of sharing his interests with others was becoming even more remote.

And during those early years the wear and tear of life were telling on his health; the nervous strain which he underwent was enormous, for, in addition to the writing of novels and political articles, he applied himself closely to study, and gave lessons to pupils. Matters were greatly complicated by the perpetual domestic difficulties which he had to encounter. It is easy to see that after his wife's death, when he was alone once more, and able to devote a few years to quiet work and social intercourse (at which time he appeared to the outer world to be placed in circumstances comparatively prosperous), his position in reality was no longer what it had been. His originally strong constitution was greatly impaired, and though health may not be able to alter the characteristics with which we are born, it undoubtedly colours our outlook upon life to an extent that we do not often realise. Such outwardly calm years as he had when living in a flat alone and writing *Isabel Clarendon*, *Demos*, *Thyrza*, and *New Grub Street*—books by which he became known—came too late, inasmuch as they came to a person made old by harassment and suffering. Gissing was, however, still the same person in one main feature—"his object in life was", as has been written of him, "to get on with his work; that achieved, he did not much care what the world at large thought of it". But "work" for him did not mean only the writing of his novels—it meant letting no day slip by without some close reading which would add to his store of knowledge. And as he read his dearly-loved Greek and Latin authors, the desire to tread the land that they had trodden, and to behold the landscape which their eyes had rested upon, became a more and more burning desire—so great, indeed, that the means of its fulfilment were soon found.

From boyhood Gissing's love of Nature was strong, but it was dimmed and clouded by the dust of many passing objects to which he had to give attention. Because his written work dealt mainly with sordid and ugly scenes, few realised that he had eyes for very different sights. The sky at sunset had for him a peculiar attraction, and countless were the vivid descriptions given of different sunsets which he had seen, and which never faded from his memory. He would not have come under the censure of Ruskin, who speaks of the disregard of the greater part of mankind for the sky, which, as he says, is for the benefit of all.

> Who saw [he asks] the dance of the dead clouds when the sunlight left them last night, and the west wind blew them before it like withered leaves? All has passed, unregretted as unseen.[1]

And the colours in which Gissing revelled, the same writer describes thus:

> The whole sky, from the zenith to the horizon, becomes one molten mantling sea of colour and fire; every black bar turns into massy gold, every ripple and wave into unsullied shadowless crimson, and purple, and scarlet, and colours for which there are no words in language, and no ideas in the mind.[2]

The sight of such skies sank deep into Gissing's mind and stayed there, as did many a lovely scene of Nature. In one of his later visits to Italy, when he marvelled at his waking moments being full of cheerfulness, he ascribed the cause to his having spent the days looking only at beautiful things.

18

No life can, indeed, be spent in looking only at what is beautiful, or in the enjoyment of complete happiness, but none can say what would have been the effect on Gissing's character could he have been spared the harrowing experiences which he brought upon himself. Never could any man have had less discernment in choosing his friends; it is therefore not surprising that his second marriage should once more have brought him infinite misery, and a renewal of the old domestic discord. He was not able, like some men, to sever himself from his responsibilities, and, forgetting his private cares, to live a life apart; for he always had an enormous sense of duty, and no personal discomfort was considered if this could be discharged. Great indeed are the difficulties to be encountered when the cares of a household fall upon one whose livelihood is entirely dependent upon his creative powers. And we have no difficulty in seeing how Gissing's powers were warped, his outlook on life in general darkened, and his health further impaired by this second unhappy union. The "aloofness from his fellow-creatures", which has been spoken of by some writers as one of his characteristics, was not his choice, but rather the result of his possessing that strange capacity for connecting himself with the wrong fellow-creatures; such a step once taken, a kind of super-sensitiveness severed him from those who would have been congenial to him. Nevertheless he was able, from time to time, to enjoy himself among his literary friends; and these were moments well spent, for he was always renewed and refreshed by such intercourse. Later on, his love for his children brought him much delight, though, in the nature of things, he could not see much of them after their early years.

But, in spite of these few pleasures, it is evident that those years of struggle produced a lasting effect upon his health. Already, when he had reached more peaceful days, and had gained by his last marriage the companionship and sympathy which he had always needed, his health was extremely delicate, and he was no longer able to withstand either the cold of winter or the heat of the summer. Those last years brought Gissing many interesting friends and many quiet days; but they brought, too, days of weakness and ill health—of visits to doctors, and of travel from place to place in search of good air which would restore to him some of his early vigour. Time spent

19

over the quiet pages of *Henry Ryecroft,* or among his beloved scenes of ancient Italy—in descriptions of Monte Casino and the cell of St. Benedict—was an enormous contrast to that spent in depicting life in Clerkenwell, or in the back streets of Lambeth, among the quarrelsome and disreputable people whose lives he had so often drawn in earlier days. Strange as it may seem, the man who wrote of these drab scenes still possessed identically the same character, but the traits which were latent in his early life gained the ascendancy, and the need for depicting all that was most harrowing, which had urged him on before, was now laid to rest. A better way was discovered for alleviating those ills—that of turning the eyes of the beholders to something that could be admired. If many critics feel that the early savage scenes were drawn with much greater force than any of those which he depicted later, and therefore represented the *real* Gissing, let them remember that it was not the strength of feeling which was lacking in this later work, but that the bodily power needed for its expression was now denied.

Was there any humour, we may ask, to light up this sombre character? Much has been said to the contrary; on the other hand, it has been pointed out that no one could have had Gissing's keen appreciation of Dickens unless he possessed some degree of humour. And if we ask whether a true sense of humour would not have touched and alleviated some of the circumstances of his life, it may perhaps be answered that his trials were of such a nature as to quench the fire of even the greatest humorist. There is no doubt that Gissing was born with a strong tendency to depression, and that this tendency was increased by too close study in his boyhood, and further deepened by the difficulties of his early manhood; but, none the less, there were times when he could be a gay companion—even an uproariously mirthful one—especially when among his favourite scenes or books. This was a side of his character practically unknown to those who knew little of him. His life, indeed, was not without its joys; his love of Nature, his keen appreciation of all that was best in literature, his enjoyment of much that was beautiful in art and in music, could not do otherwise than bring hours of far more solid satisfaction than come to many whose lives we call happy and successful. To see and to know Gissing at these times was to forget entirely those

epithets which are continually attached to his name—
"gloomy", "pessimistic", "tragic". To no other writer have
such terms been so persistently applied, to the complete
exclusion of the brighter side. Not all of Gissing's books were of
a miserable type. *The Town Traveller* and *The Paying Guest*
contain a good deal of amusement; and others, such as *The
Crown of Life, Our Friend the Charlatan, Will Warburton, Veranilda,*
and *Henry Ryecroft,* are far from gloomy.

Many questions have been asked somewhat petulantly as to
the cause of Gissing's melancholy outlook. Wounded vanity, a
lack of the good things of life, dislike of his fellow-men—each
has been suggested as a solution; but in reality the cause lay in
none of these. The conduct of his life was marked by a series of
rash steps, which led to prolonged unhappiness, and produced
a lasting impression upon his acutely sensitive temperament,
depriving him of the many joys to which his heart and mind
were peculiarly alive. In this we have the secret of Gissing's
melancholy outlook.

Throughout all the contradictions of his character,
paradoxical though it may sound, there runs a certain
unmistakable consistency; and though, in one sense, we might
be said never to know what such a man would do, yet on the
other hand it would be true to say that we knew what he would
not do. For, in this strange misshapen life, there was a central
cord which held all the parts together; there was a principle
deeply embedded in his nature which caused him to prefer that
he himself should suffer rather than bring suffering upon others;
and in this lay the secret of the life which to outsiders appeared
only steeped in gloom, but out of which, for those who knew
him, there shone a gleam of imperishable gold.

NOTES

1 Ruskin, *Modern Painters,* vol. i.
2 *Ibid.*

2

George Gissing

by AUSTIN HARRISON*

One evening, late in the year 1882, two very small boys were sitting on the stairs in a London house, junketing merrily on an assortment of viands and delicacies purloined from the dining-room, where a dinner party was proceeding, yet with much dread in the inner man. For the first time in their lives stern reality fronted them. On the morrow at 9 a.m. they were to begin a life by initiation into the past. The golden age was over, the gossamer reign of licit irresponsibility; they were to have a tutor. No wonder if a few tears—the last tears of babyhood—fell sympathetically into the champagne glass beside them. The talk was of thwackings and impositions.

Punctually to the minute on the next day the front door bell rang. How vividly I can recall the agony of suspense ensuing! My brother, who even at that age was ever drawing, broke his slate pencil; we rose as the door opened, and there walked into the room one of the gentlest looking beings we had ever seen. With the instinctive perception of children we measured our man at a glance. Before the lesson began we had both ceased to fear him, long before it was finished he had become a dear friend. He talked to us of the Greeks and Romans with boisterous enthusiasm; gave us quaint Latin terminations to our names, and we, struck by his gentleness and the singular pathos of his countenance, retorted with "Gissinus-y

* "George Gissing" by Austin Harrison: reprinted from *Nineteenth Century*, LX, September 1906, pp. 453-63.

creature"—and as such he was known to us to the very end.

Tall, spare, and lissom of movement, George Gissing had a marked personality even then. Here is a conscious autobiographical portrait of himself taken from his first novel, *Workers in the Dawn*. "His eyes were of light blue, his nose was of a Grecian type, his lips and chin were moulded in form expressive of extreme sensibility and gentleness of disposition, showing traces, moreover, of instability in moral character". Thick, brown hair clustered round a brow of noble shape; his head was well shaped. Though his cheeks lacked colour he looked healthy, strong and vigorous. His facial expression was extraordinarily mobile, sensitive, and intellectual. I have never seen so sad and pathetic a face. In repose his features contracted into a look of ineffable dreariness, sorrow and affliction, of mute submissiveness and despair. Yet it was a noble face, dignified, delicate, sensuous, thoughtful. And then it would flash and light up, and the eyes would beam in radiant transport, and the misanthrope would become a tempestuous schoolboy, and he would thump the table and positively shout with buoyant exuberance. For there was ever laughter in his heart—spontaneous, boisterous, sincere laughter. Gissing, the sad man, had the zest of life, and with it its joy. At times he would laugh so uproariously at lessons that my father, at work in the adjoining-room, would come in to see what was amiss. And the Homeric joke would be repeated and we would all laugh the louder and merrier.

Let me say at once that it is no purpose of mine to lift the veil of mystery overhanging Mr. Gissing's life, to disturb what Michelet called *le désintéressement des morts*. Gissing's life was an infinitely sad, an infinitely pathetic one. To him it was decreed: "Thou shalt live alone." In the bitter years of pursuit and attainment he wrought literally in solitude, unknown. He had but one friend, an author like himself, whom he saw at rare intervals. He chose to live fiercely independent, proud and resentful, at war with the whole social organism. For years he was a kind of literary miser, spurning mankind, scorning sympathy: he, one of the kindest, gentlest natures that" ever breathed, with his soul bared to the lash of circumstance. Fate made him a ferocious individualist. The world frightened him, and, as he himself says somewhere, "a frightened man is no

good for anything". His repining spirit trod its own Calvary.
Legend has been both kind and unkind. It has woven a
convention around his life, derived in the main from the
autobiographical nature of his writings: in part fictitious, in
part too grossly misleading and fantastic. The man whom none
knew in life is now crowned with the wreath of posthumous
compassion. Extremes lead to extremes. And so it has come
about that Gissing has gone down to posterity as a man whose
life was consumed in the reek of slum and garret, who for twenty
years starved literally in the nether world of our great capital.
As it was my privilege to have known Gissing from the very
outset of his literary career and to have remained in more or less
unbroken relationship with him till his sad death at St. Jean-de-
Luz two years ago, perhaps I may be permitted to correct the
perspective of certain erroneous impressions which it can now
serve no useful purpose to maintain.

As a boy Gissing had been the prodigy of his school; he
worked madly (as Mr. Wells has said[1]); "already out of touch
with life", a lonely portent. From there he went to Owens
College, Manchester, where in a career of meteoric brilliance he
carried off all the first prizes, scholarships and exhibitions, and
took first-class honours for English and classics in the
University of London. From that time "his is a broken and
abnormal career".[2] It matters little now. Suffice it to say that at
the height of a young life of quite unusual promise one of those
aberrations of mental balance took place which in men of
genius, alas! is by no means uncommon, and that the penalty
was severe and, in Gissing's case, decisive upon his whole
future. As he himself wrote many years later: "Within my
nature there seemed to be no faculty of self-guidance."[3] The
boy was dead. His life's struggle began. He fled to America.
There he taught the classics for a space, dabbled a little in print,
but his fierce spirit could find no rest; he broke away from the
restraint of cities, roved penniless through the States, racked
and distraught, and at last stood before the majesty of Niagara
hesitating, as he often related to us, between life and death. He
returned and went to Germany.

He taught and studied. In the quiet atmosphere of a German
university town he found guidance and inspiration. He read
Schiller, Goethe, Häckel, Schopenhauer, innumerable German

GEORGE GISSING

tomes on ancient philosophy, Lucian, Petronius, and what not.
In *Workers in the Dawn* he has left a faithful record of his own
mind-growth. From Schopenhauer he turned to Comte, whose
"Philosophie Positive" profoundly impressed him. His leisure
hours he spent in conversations with a learned German, at the
time *Privat-docent,* with whom he remained in life-long
friendship. The two young men discussed metaphysics and
religion with German thoroughness and system. At one period
he nearly became a Catholic. "Yes, how much have I to thank
Germany for," he writes in *Workers in the Dawn.* "I came here
with a mind rudely ploughed by the ploughshare of anguish ...
How well I remember the day when I took up Strauss's *Leben
Jesu.* The book was to me like the first ray of heavenly light
piercing the darkness of a night of anguish and striving and woe
unutterable". Hope returned to him. He acquired merit; he
learnt the joy of struggling with the world. "At no stage in its
struggle is a human mind contemptible," he wrote; "for as long
as it does struggle it asserts its native nobility, its inherent
principle of life."

> Schopenhauer, Comte, and Shelley—these three in turn have
> directed the growth of my moral life. Schopenhauer taught me to
> forget myself and to live in others. Comte then came to me with
> his lucid unfolding of the mystery of the world, and taught me the
> use to which my sympathy should be directed. Last of all Shelley
> breathed with the breath of life on the dry bones of scientific
> theory, turned conviction into passion, lit the heavens of the
> future with such glorious rays that the eye struggles in gazing
> upwards, strengthened the heart with enthusiasm as with a coat
> of mail[4]

And again:

> With a heart full of noble phantasies and lofty aspirations;
> beating high with an all-embracing affection for earth and the
> children of earth, bred of a natural ardour of disposition, and
> nurtured upon the sweet and mighty thoughts of great man; with
> a heart yearning for action of some kind, weary of a life bounded
> within the lines of self-study, desirous of nothing more than to
> efface the recollection of self in complete devotion to the needs of
> those sufferers.

Gissing set foot once more in England. He had come to the

conclusion that the true destination of philosophy must be social and practical; he determined to write. The result was *Workers in the Dawn,* a crude, incondite work in three volumes— in some ways the most powerful book he ever wrote. I have quoted from it because it is an unknown work and because it reveals the true Gissing of that time, the aching soul of torment and desire, the artist and pessimist. It is admittedly partly autobiographical. The hero, finding the world void and remorseless, plunges into the waters of Niagara. The writing is curiously raw and amateurish, which is instructive, as Gissing was then a scholar of real distinction, and was shortly to become one of the few great living writers of prose in the English language. Very few people have ever seen this book. Gissing, it so happened, had inherited the sum of one hunded pounds, and with this he published his first novel. But in those days there were no literary agents, and Gissing was an unknown scribe. He laughed long and loud when the bill came in for printing an edition of his book, which left him with a few shillings in his pocket. Only a few copies were sold; he was now face to face with hunger and destitution.

He sent the book to my father and, I think, to Mr. John Morley. Both agreed as to its power and interest. An interview followed; my father was deeply impressed with the forlorn figure of the young scholar and writer, and so by a fortunate coincidence my brother and I gained a tutor, and the tutor a livelihood. Gissing taught us from that day uninterruptedly till the autumn of the year 1884; and I make claim to affirm that from that moment the story of Gissing starving in garret and cellar, swinking all day and night with lard and dripping for his nourishment and the wooden boards for his pillow, is the fiction of fiction. A poor man certainly he was, but from the year 1882 Gissing never "starved", as he is commonly represented to have done. Through us he taught a son of Mr. Montague Crackenthorpe, K.C., the daughters of Mr. Vernon Lushington, and various other pupils whose names need not be mentioned. What is worth noting is that from the year 1882— two years before, that is, Gissing's first novel, *The Unclassed,* appeared—he was in receipt of a livable income derivable from teaching, which he could always increase or modify at will, and that for some years subsequently he did exist by this form of journeywork, while devoting the whole of his leisure and industry to novel writing. The sickness of real poverty Gissing never knew after the year 1882, when his literary career in fact began. Previously, without doubt, he had experienced very rough times—in America, where he nearly starved, and later in London on his return from Germany. What I wish to point out is not that Gissing was not a poor man; not that he did not suffer physically and mentally; not that his whole life was not more or less of a struggle to make two ends meet, but that after the publication of *The Unclassed,* and subsequently during the whole of his literary career, he was not the necessitous starving writer convention has depicted him; not in any true sense of the word the literary jetsam of garret and cellar tossed hither and thither by poverty and hunger in the grim immensity of London. When Gissing lived in Milton Street, in Chelsea, behind Madame Tussaud's, at Cornwall Residences and elsewhere, from 1882 to 1890, my brother and I used frequently to visit him, and great times we had together; great teas, great talks and laughter. Sometimes we would drop in unexpectedly, and find Gissing and his friend in the fever of literary conversation, smoking and drinking pint after pint of tea. Sometimes we would go for long tramps with him to Harrow or Kew, and without ceasing Gissing would talk of his work and experiences, shouting with laughter at some of his stories of life in what he called "the glorious black depths of London", and on such occasions he would race us, walking or running with boyish zest and agility.

To tell the truth, in all practical things Gissing was idle and inept. He had in marked degree the artistic temper; if he remained poor it was largely because he chose to. My father introduced him to Mr. John Morley, at the time editor of the *Pall Mall,* who published a charming sketch of Gissing's, "On Battersea Bridge". We implored him to write again. But Gissing refused. He hated editors; he was no journalist, he said; he could not degrade himself by such "trash". In truth, at any time after 1882, Gissing could have enabled him to write at leisure. But he would never hear of such a thing. My father begged him to accept some post, but Gissing declined to "serve". Gissing positively chose to live in strife. He writes a pathetic note to my mother, the 6th of July, 1884:

A kind of exhaustion possesses me when I sit at my desk a quarter of an hour, and my will power gets weaker. At most I am able to produce a short poem now and then of a very savage character. Of course all this means that the conditions of my life are preposterous. There is only one consolation, that, if I live through it, I shall have materials for darker and stronger work than any our time has seen. If I can hold out till I have written some three or four books, I shall at all events have the satisfaction of knowing that I have left something too individual in tone to be neglected.

After that he went with us for three weeks to Bonscale in the Lakes.

Really Gissing's trouble was himself; he made his own poverty; he could not be practical. He used to fall into fits of despondency and gloom, when he would sally out into the streets, and walk through the night. He was an outrageous pessimist. Four days in the week he would write from nine in the evening till four a.m., and on the fifth day he would marvel that what he called the "bilious fever" had fallen upon him. It was not that Gissing was so poor—many a German student, and the mother of many an officer of nobility in the German Army, have less than Gissing had to live on—but that in all affairs of the world he was a very child, with a child's obstinacy and improvidence.

Here, in a letter addressed to my father, the 17th of August, 1884, Milton Street, is the Gissing of that period. My father was anxious that Gissing should take up the tuition of my two younger brothers, as my brother and I were going to school. He writes:

"With reference to your proposal concerning the little boys. Should you in very deed think that I can be of use with them I need not say how unreservedly I offer myself for the work. On the other hand, should the suggestion have originated only in kind forethought for myself, I have a sort of feeling that possibly it would be better for me to burn my ships, and commence in down-right earnest the combat with the beasts of Ephesus—otherwise, with publishers in London—an absurdly mixed metaphor, by the way. Moreover, when young . . . [another pupil] went away, his father distinctly asked me if I should be able to resume work in October so that almost a livelihood would

be assured in that way for some months. . . I have plans of all
kinds—for a play, for articles, etc. Some day I shall of course look
back with sad amusement at these initial struggles—and with
keen enough feelings towards all who helped me.

So that in the year 1884 we find Gissing declining further
pupils on the ground that for the time being a livelihood was
assured him. *The Unclassed* had already appeared.

Gissing was an artist; a contemplative individualist; a man
influenced by the mood of the sky, the procession of the year; by
circumstance and environment. To understand and even to
sympathise fully with him one must remember that all his hopes
and ambitions had been shattered at the most impressionist
period of his life; that he had been shipwrecked, as it were, at the
outset of his progress in the world; and that, as a consequence,
the youth had been transformed into a hard and bitter man. By
nature he was made for the life of tranquility and meditation, for
cultured leisure and repose. Constitutionally he was an idealist,
a dreamer, an impressionist, a scholar. In other circumstances
he might have been a university don, a famous scholar, have
amassed learning and fame. He worshipped the old, the dusty
volumes of dead languages; vellum and parchment. I have seen
him take up a worm-eaten copy of an old chronicle or Greek
author and caress it as a child will stroke the coat of some fond
animal. A library was to him a garden of roses; he loved books as
women love flowers: emotionally, instinctively. He had a
Grecian love for all beauty.

But in truth Gissing looked, and had to look, back upon
beginnings of life deformed and discoloured. Unlike other men,
he practically began life with no disillusions to face. He came to
London in a spirit of pride and revolt which struggled to find
expression. Gissing was no philosopher, no Socialist reformer,
he was not even a profound thinker. He was, as he himself says,
an "egoist in grain". He deliberately regarded himself as a sort
of social outlaw, making a virtue of self-indulgence and self-
concentration, fostering the hunger of querulous self-pity. He
gloried in the vanity of self-compassion. In literature he thought
of poverty in *avoirdupois*. He revelled in the gloom of London's
misery. Every fibre of him betrayed the artist, and because he
was an artist he was also an aristocrat. His delight in poverty, in

misery, and in vice was purely artistic and consciously egoistical. His social enthusiasm was purely literary, emotional, artistic. In *The Unclassed* he laid bare his confessions. "The zeal," he writes, "on behalf of the suffering masses was nothing more nor less than disguised zeal on behalf of my own starved passions." He passed rapidly through the phases of Socialism, Radicalism, philanthropic enthusiasm.

> I have only to go out into the streets all night to come across half a hundred scenes of awful suffering or degradation, every one of which fills me with absolute joy. Think you Hogarth would have rejoiced in the destruction of Gin Lane? Never believe it! . . . My artistic egotism bids fair to ally itself with vulgar selfishness. I am often tempted to believe that one great work of art embodying human misery would be ample justification of the whole world's anguish.[5]

And in the same way Gissing took an artistic pleasure in physical pain. This body is but as the cottage or clothing of the mind. "Let flesh be racked," he writes in *Henry Ryecroft*. "I, the very I, will stand apart, lord of myself." Once, I can recall, Gissing was suffering from severe toothache, and my mother urged him to have the tooth taken out with gas. But Gissing would not hear of such a thing. He wished to feel pain, and on the next day at luncheon he gave us a vivid description of the agony he had endured. Thus his vision was blighted, and his mind soured. He scorned the carpet-author, writing at leisure on a fat salary. He loved to flesh his satire upon the lad entering the literary profession with "parental approval and ready avuncular support". His whole soul reluctant at the idea of leisured literary conception. He wrote, thought, and lived as an artist. As an artist he must be judged.

Listen to Gissing on the people in the dress of Henry Ryecroft:

> I am no friend of the people. As a force, by which the tenor of the time is conditioned, they inspire me with distrust, with fear; as a visible multitude, they make me shrink aloof, and often move me to abhorrence . . . Every instinct of my being is anti-democratic, and I dread to think of what our England may become when Demos rules irresistibly.

Sentiments, those, of a pure aristocrat, yet written in the

mellow serenity of age, when his life's work was done. I wrote to him on reading those words, and this is what he answered in a letter written at Ciboure late in the summer of 1903, a few months before his death:

> Of a truth, I did not mean to be hard upon the poor. There are human sweepings in London and elsewhere, with which I hold no terms of kindliness but "the poor"—the decent, hard-working man or woman who will never know what it is to feel secure of next month's food and lodging, with them I sympathise profoundly. I do not say that we should get on well together—we should not; but that is my fault as much as theirs.

In a letter to my father (29th of June, 1884) Gissing makes some interesting remarks about himself:

> Surely, there is a sense wanting in me. . . I feel the irresistible impulse to strive after my ideal of artistic excellence. It is true, as you said, that I have a quarrel with society, and that, I suppose, explains the instinct. But the quarrel is life-long; ever since I can remember I have known this passionate tendency of revolt. It has sought for satisfaction in many schools and many modes of life. I write these social passages in a fury; but I scribbled in precisely the same temper when I was ten years old. If only I could hear someone speak a word for a tendency which in me is an instinct! I must ask you to let me try to express something of the gratitude I feel for your persistent kindness—kindness holding on in spite of everything.

The secret of Gissing's life was that his was an ill-balanced nature, lacking in firmness and volition. By constitution of mind an idealist, he was dependent upon external influences for the shape which his idealism should for the time assume. If noble impulse directed his activity, adverse circumstance forbade the implanted seeds from growing into a rich individuality. Yet Gissing was very English. He hated Pecksniff, and, though he described his countrymen as an Old Testament people, he was himself very insular in many things, and a bit of a Philistine. His hatred of parsimony, poverty; his almost snobbish respect for social position, his hyper-sensitiveness to his own; his shrinkage into scorn of his fellow-creatures; his fierce spirit of independence, intolerance; his love of air, and freedom, and nature; his shyness—though no man ever lived with a greater capacity for mirth; his love of comfort, hatred of control, discipline, pity and protection; his narrowness of vision, his yearning for sympathy while savagely refusing it—all these are English characteristics which Gissing had in marked degree.

A gentler nature, a more delightful companion than Gissing never existed. Both my brother and I were lazy and impish enough, yet Gissing never, during the course of two years' instruction, punished us. Once only, when, in imitation of frogs, we both chanted an Aristophanic chorus, seated on the table and declined to move or desist, did Gissing lose his patience. He rose, put on his hat, and strode in silence from the room and house. After that his every wish was, I am glad to think now, piously obeyed. As tutor he took a personal interest in both of us. Himself a good draughtsman, he encouraged my brother's marked artistic gifts, gave him his first sketch-book and his first lessons in perspective, and drew in it a sea piece, which my brother has to this day. In those days I wrote plays, and my brother painted the scenery. On one occasion we gave a grand performance at which Gissing was present. Its reception seemed doubtful until the High Priest said:

> I, a holy man, am not a fool,
> Often as a boy along a pool, etc. . .

which brought down the house. Gissing burst into a paroxysm of laughter, and continued laughing for fully ten minutes. All joined in; the success of the piece was assured. He used often subsequently to quote that line, and on each occasion he would laugh and shout with glee. Gissing was very fond of whistling too—in a peculiarly low and gentle tone. His favourite air was "Twickenham Ferry". After nearly every lesson he had to whistle it for us, and he would always end with the words, "Yes, it is very beautiful". Reverential was his love for music. He has told in *Ryecroft* how the barrel organs "tuned" his thoughts, and in a fine passage he describes how once his racked mind was quieted by the strains of a piano in Eaton Square.

Pictures and music always afforded him a keen, almost ecstatic pleasure. I have seen him sit, when my mother was playing Chopin or Bach, with tears welling in his eyes. At such moments he would remain quite motionless. The sound of music seemed to stun and soothe him. Art, all forms of beauty, influenced him strangely, physically. In one of his London lodgings he lived above a well-known composer of waltzes, who never ceased from troubling and thrumming. Yet Gissing was happy; as he said, "it made the words flow".

He was extremely fond of cats. His solace and companion for some years was Grim—a big black common Tom, his lonely confidant. To Grim he would discourse aloud, of Grim he would talk to us as of an old and dear friend. When Grim one day went the way of other Toms, Gissing quite broke down, and he wrote an elegy to its memory. Gissing was no mean poet. In the summer of 1883, when my grandmother lived at Sutton Place, he used to come down three times a week to teach us in the mornings, and sometimes after luncheon he would stay and sit in the punt on the river and write poems. One of these was called "Only a Cigarette". It was a dainty ode to a girl he had seen smoking, lazily reclining on the river-bank. He wrote, too, a powerful poem to "The Little Childen"—both of which, unfortunately, I have lost. But I can see him now, sitting on the table in the long tapestried gallery at Sutton reciting verses with his voice and look of artistic enthusiasm.

Like all men of deep feeling and emotion, Gissing adored the sun and nature. Later in life, when he had shaken the dust of London for ever off his feet, he found in the contemplation of nature what the city had never given him—peace and contentment. Of the sun he writes finely in *Ryecroft:* "I went bare-headed, that the golden beams of the sun might shed upon me their unstinted blessing." He learnt, too, the beauty of flowers; like his father, he became an enthusiastic botanist. He is speaking in *Ryecroft:*

> To me flowers became symbolical of a great release, of a wonderful awakening. I recall my moments of delight, the recognition of each flower that unfolded, the surprise of budding branches clothed in a night with green. Meadows shining with buttercups, hollows sunned with the marsh marigold, held me long at gaze. I saw the sallow glistening with its cones of silvery fur and splendid with dust of gold. These common things touch me with more admiration and of wonder each time I behold them. As I turn to summer, a misgiving mingles with my joy.

33

I well remember a walk I had with Gissing about the year 1895 on the Blackdown Hill near Haslemere. The townsman I had known as a child had become a passionate lover of the country. His hair was brushed back over his forehead like a musician; he was full with the enthusiasm of old days. His knowledge of flowers and plants was extraordinary. The purple heather, the moorland waste, the sense of loneliness and expanse delighted him. He picked up a little plant and explained its life and structure with the scientific knowledge of a botanist. Every fern and wild flower stirred him to rapture and to fresh discourse.

When Gissing went with us to Bonscale in 1884 he was rampageous as any schoolboy. He would row for hours on Ullswater lake, but his great joy was the Hills. All day he would tramp, sometimes with us up Helvellyn, and sometimes alone. One walk especially I remember his taking from Patterdale to Ambleside through Rysdale to Grasmere and back over Grisedale. His great joy was to lie on his back at the top of a hill and apostrophise the cairn. And coming down he was as fleet as an Alpine guide. Sometimes we would make him play cricket; and as for climbing trees, Gissing was up at the top branch before we could get a hold of the lowest. He was strong in his arms and could climb a rope like a sailor. Killing animals, hunting, sport of all kind he abominated. But he would walk all day through any weather; he had Ruskin's passion for hills.

Gissing was not a good conversationalist. For that he lived too much alone. He loved silence and solitude; he hated noise, the clamour of the human voice. Once we took him to a garden party at the country residence of Lady ——. Gissing sat on a chair in the corner of the room, mute and dejected. The cackle and scream of idiot mirth rendered him speechless. He sat for an hour for all the world like the figure of a wet bird, amid the rustle of silk and chiffon, and never smiled till we left the house. Society unnerved him. But on the hills, or in sympathetic company, Gissing was a wonderful talker, wildly enthusiastic, suggestive, imaginative, and the words would flow in torrents from his mouth. On Homer, Shakespeare, art and poetry, Gissing rose to flights of rhetoric. Once he had a great discussion on patriotism with the late Mlle. Souvestre. She cited the case of Henri Regnault, who returned from Algiers to fight in the Siege of Paris, as a crowning example of noble, patriotism. All Gissing's artist's feelings were aflame. He would not hear of it. Regnault was an artist—art the supreme thing in life; the Siege of Paris was not worth an artist's life. I don't think Gissing had much sense of humour, and he certainly was not witty. He took himself and life too seriously; he never got out of himself, never got beyond the littleness of the great I. It was years before his mind grew mellow with the calm of dignified reflection.

In no way should *Ryecroft* be regarded as an autobiography. "The thing," he wrote to my father, 11th of February, 1903, "is much more an aspiration than a memory. I hope too much will not be made of the few autobiographical papers in the book." To me it seems by far the maturest of his works, full of golden words and thoughts and fancies. His life was rounded; the end, he knew, was not far distant. "They tell me that at my peril I shall try to live elsewhere—yet I hope to see Italy again before I die," he wrote to me three months before his death. "Does it seem long to you, the old days of Latin Grammar? To me, very, very long—I was strong then, and could do anything." Gissing was no patriot in the political sense of the word; politics he hated and despised, but I doubt if any man wrote about Shakespeare and his country in words more noble than these:

> Among the many reasons which make me glad to have been born in England, one of the first is that I read Shakespeare in my mother tongue . . . Let every land have joy of its poet; for the poet is the land itself, all its greatness and its sweetness, all that incommunicable heritage for which men live and die. As I close the book, love and reverence possess me. Whether does my full heart turn to the great Enchanter, or to the Island upon which he has laid his spell? I know not. I cannot think of them apart. In the love and reverence awakened by that voice of voices, Shakespeare and England are but one.[6]

Those who knew Gissing can never forget him. His was a life of bitter endurance, of toil and trial, of sombre tragedy. His was no vain endeavour, no mock enthusiasm. A weak vessel—a lofty intelligence, a noble mind, a sincere and beautiful nature—the words of Goethe seem fitting as an epitaph:

> *Wer nie sein Brod mit Tränen ass,*
> *Wer nie die kummervollen Nächte*

Auf seinem Bette weinend sass,
Der kennt euch nicht, ihr himmlischen Mächte.

NOTES

1 *Monthly Review*, August 1904.
2 *Ibid.*
3 *Henry Ryecroft.*
4 *Workers in the Dawn.*
5 *The Unclassed.*
6 *Henry Ryecroft.*

3

The Vitality of George Gissing

by ROBERT SHAFER*

Gissing's fiction indisputably possesses a vitality which has given the man a secure position amongst the nine or ten English novelists of the nineteenth century who wrote not alone for their own time or place. Interest in Gissing has been very active continuously since his death in December, 1903, and has, indeed, notably increased in recent years. This is attested not only by animated critical discussion but, more impressively, by a steady growing demand for his books. About seventeen of these either have been kept in print continuously since their first publication or have been reprinted, some of them in more than one edition and on both sides of the Atlantic, during the last ten or fifteen years. Such a fact speaks plainly enough for itself; though it does not mean that Gissing, never in his lifetime a popular writer, is at all likely now or in the future to become the object of extremely widespread eager acclamation.

When *Workers in the Dawn* appeared in 1880—the first of Gissing's novels to achieve publication, although not the first to be written—it found certainly less than fifty readers, including the reviewers. These gentlemen found little in it worthy of their attention, some condemning it severely for its crudity, others for subversive tendencies they discovered in it. Amongst readers, however, there were at least two, Frederic Harrison and John Morley, who thought it extraordinarily powerful despite all

* "The Vitality of George Gissing" by Robert Shafer: reprinted from *The American Review*, 1935, pp. 459-87.

artistic shortcomings. They were in fact so struck by the downright genuineness of the novel that they exerted themselves to do everything they could for the rather strange young man—he was then not quite twenty-three years old—who had written it; and Frederic Harrison really set him on his feet, rescuing him from something close to gradual starvation and giving him a means of livelihood with leisure not merely for a somewhat human way of life but for continued writing as well.

The circumstance is worth recalling, because it is fairly typical of Gissing's whole career, and also of his posthumous fortunes. He wrote in all twenty-five novels (though three of these were never printed), a great many short stories, the best critical study of Dickens that we have or are likely ever to have, a set of critical introductions to Dickens's novels, a wholly delightful volume of travel sketches, and a book defying classification by which he is now, I suppose, most widely known, *The Private Papers of Henry Ryecroft.* And throughout the quarter of a century while these many books were being composed and published, he had a slowly growing audience impressed by his work very much as Frederic Harrison and Morley had been—feeling that here was a fine and sensitive intelligence succeeding against odds in the creation of powerfully conceived and executed pictures of life, pictures evidently authentic, perhaps imperishable, certainly challenging, whose dark significance could not be denied or belittled. Probably no one ever thought that the truth mirrored by Gissing could be received by the generality of readers; but that an audience was gradually found and was kept is proved by the fact that after *Workers in the Dawn* Gissing published no book which did not pay its way and yield some profit, and that after his first ten years of work he had a solid reputation which brought him during the remainder of his life more proposals from publishers than he could take up.

One may say, of course, that here is evidence of modest commercial success but not, necessarily, of anything else; and it is true that though Gissing, during his lifetime and since, has had devoted champions amongst critics, he has also had critical enemies, who have insisted that his books are worthless or worse, that his novels prove he was not a novelist, whatever he was, and that they are really dead and should be buried. Thus, to take the latest instance which has come to hand of the reaction dictated by reigning prejudices, Mr. H.G. Wells, who was a personal friend of Gissing during the last seven years of the latter's life, has dedicated some pages to a brief account of the man in his *Experiment in Autobiography*, published towards the end of 1934; and this is the kind of thing he says:

> The Gissing I knew. . . was an extraordinary blend of a damaged joy-loving human being hampered by inherited gentility and a classical education. He craved to laugh, jest, enjoy, stride along against a wind, shout, "quaff mighty flagons". But his upbringing. . . had been one of repressive gentility, where "what will the neighbours *think* of us?" was more terrible than the thunder of God. The insanity of our educational organization had. . . poured into that fresh and vigorous young brain nothing but classics and a "scorn" for nonclassical things. Gissing's imagination, therefore, escaped from the cramping gentilities and respectability of home to find its compensations in the rhetorical swagger, the rotundities and the pompous grossness of Rome. He walked about. . . in love with goddesses and nymphs and excited by ideas of patrician freedoms in a world of untouchable women. . . Gissing was a Latin, oratorical and not scientific, unanalytical, unsubtle and secretly haughty. He accepted and identified himself with all the pretensions of Rome's triumphal arches. . . Some of his books will be read for many generations, but because of this warping of his mind they will find fewer lovers than readers. . . Through Gissing I was confirmed in my suspicion that. . . orthodox classical training. . . is. . . no longer a city of refuge from barbaric predispositions. . . That disposition to get away from entangling conditions which is manifest in almost every type of imaginative worker, accumulated in his case to quite desperate fugitive drives. . . Perhaps Gissing was made to be hunted by Fate. He never turned and fought. He always hid or fled. . . He was a pessimistic writer. He spent his big fine brain depreciating life, because he would not and perhaps could not look life squarely in the eyes— neither his circumstances nor the conventions about him nor the adverse things about him nor the limitations of his personal character.

Mr. Wells sinks into unwonted hesitation at the close of his sketch, confessing that he does not know whether it was nature or the insanities of classical education which ruined Gissing's "big fine brain". Mr. Wells's monstrous and sometimes amusing prejudices, which throughout, as I have intimated above, are more in evidence than any true observation of his friend, strongly incline him to accuse education; yet he refers with unqualified approval to Mr. Frank Swinnerton's critical study of Gissing, where the trouble with the poor fellow is ascribed to egotism "of a particular kind". Gissing, Mr. Swinnerton says, was "temperamentally unhappy":

> He did not love his fellow men. He had suffered much, and he was, during the greater part of his life, expressing his suffering in terms of his distaste. For that reason, although he is often mentioned by those who write about novels, he is not very much read by the fashionable; and indeed at the present time I believe the greatest readers of his books are to be found less among those who can appreciate their value than among those who find in the novels an expression of their own bitter and egotistical hostility to life. He is thus, if I am right, helping discontent to arise in the mediocre. It is not that he had any liking for mediocrity—he hated it; nor that his books are addressed to stupid people. But in the nature of things his books will be increasingly read by ill-educated egoists, because they voice numerous dislikes—of the vulgar herd, of conventional Christians, and so on—which are capable of flattering a sense of superiority in miscultured readers. The ideas he expressed have, as it were, percolated through the strata of intellectual and intelligent people, and they are now food for the agitated lower middle-class. Accordingly, it is among members of that class that Gissing is at present finding his most constant readers.

Neither Mr. Wells nor Mr. Swinnerton is unable to see *any* merit or enduring value in Gissing's work, but both of them, it will be agreed, are far indeed from a German critic and historian of English literature who has declared that next to Thomas Hardy, Gissing is the most significant man of letters to be found in England in the latter part of the nineteenth century.[1] And this German critic's verdict is only one in a long series scarcely less favourable which could be cited from England, from the United States, and from continental Europe; while I myself, if I may say so, believe that Gissing is a more significant and, in a real sense, more important writer than Hardy, though far below him as an artist.

40

Now a sharp conflict of critical opinion, such as Gissing has occasioned and still occasions, is itself no uncertain indication of vitality in a man's books, giving them a power which may attract or repel, but which cannnot be ignored. There was, to take the most celebrated instance, a long critical battle over Shakespeare. Many writers of the seventeenth and eighteenth centuries spoke of him with strong disapproval, some of them believing practically what Mr. Swinnerton today believes of Gissing—that Shakespeare, if he continued long to have any appeal, could attract only the vulgar and ill-educated kind of reader.

Gissing, however, was no second Shakespeare; and in this transparent fact we discover the real critical problem which he forces upon us. Gissing's insight was very far from universal; his imagination was neither easily kindled, nor bold, nor sure; he had none of that exuberant energy which sparkles from the pages of *Romeo and Juliet,* and *A Midsummer Night's Dream* and *As You Like It,* and which still glows, subdued but intense and magnificent, in *Othello* and *Hamlet;* he brings before his readers no thronging gallery of characters of every kind and rank, impelling them to feel that here is God's plenty, here is all humanity in its richness and greatness and wonder and absurdity and misery. In fact Gissing was almost always a very imperfect, and always a very limited artist, with a small canvas, with not many colours—and those not the most striking or vivid—with a blunt pencil which sometimes failed to do his bidding, and with an eye which saw truly only a few kinds of people, and which saw during the greater part of his career predominantly the more grim and misery-provoking aspects of existence. He himself in *The Private Papers of Henry Ryecroft* suggested that "one might define Art as an expression, satisfying and abiding, of the zest of life". But, as Mr. Paul More has remarked, by this standard not one of Gissing's novels could be regarded as a successful work of art. Generally speaking, the atmosphere of the novels is one of dreariness and defeat, and Gissing seems to be animated by disgust and contempt rather than by anything even remotely like the zest of life. In saying above that his novels cannot be expected ever to become popular, howsoever highly they may be valued, I had in mind this fact, that they present us with much that is calculated to depress and sadden us, and to make us wonder whether life itself may not be irremidiably senseless and hopeless.

Clearly then Mr. Wells and Mr. Swinnerton and others who have joined them in the indictment of Gissing can make out a strong case; and indeed Gissing was beforehand with them and by anticipation himself agreed with their verdict. It was he who first said that he was a faltering artist and a novelist only under compulsion; and a year before his death he wrote in a letter, with reference to *The Private Papers of Henry Ryecroft*: "On the whole I suspect it is the best thing I have done or am likely to do; the thing most likely to last when all my other futile work has followed my futile life." This conviction of failure or defeat can, as we shall see, be explained, and does not rightly mean what it seems to. Nevertheless, there it is, rendering only the more complex and insistent the problem of accounting for Gissing's vitality.

2

In attempting the task it is needful first to turn to the book I have already referred to several times, *The Private Papers of Henry Ryecroft*. This is a work of fiction, and Ryecroft, the ostensible writer, is not Gissing; yet Gissing here, as in a number of his novels, drew heavily upon his own experience and gave form to his own thought. Hence it is possible, and in this case neither difficult nor hazardous, to unweave the fabric and so to obtain a picture, incomplete but authentic as far as it goes, of the kind of man Gissing became by the time he was about forty years old.

The dominant characteristic of the volume is its serenity. The man not obscurely reflected in its pages is at peace with himself and with the world; tranquilly accepting life as it comes, almost as a disinterested spectator; detached from nearly every worldly concern that harasses or enslaves the great majority of us; yet not stupidly or coldly indifferent; keenly delighted, on the contrary, by even the simplest of the fair aspects of nature, of humanity, of civilization; frankly in love with the southern English countryside, and indeed with all things genuinely and honestly English, not degraded, as he thinks English life and the English character are being degraded, by the corrupt influence of industrialism. His love for honest English cooking is

42

unqualified and touching, in fact almost convincing. And he is strongly of the right mind about vegetarianism. In the literature of this subject, he says, there is "an odd pathos":

> I remember the day when I read these periodicals and pamphlets with all the zest of hunger and poverty, vigorously seeking to persuade myself that flesh was an altogether superfluous, and even a repulsive, food. If ever such things fall under my eyes nowadays, I am touched with a half-humorous compassion for the people whose necessity, not their will, consents to this chemical view of diet. There comes before me a vision of certain vegetarian restaurants, where, at a minimum outlay, I have often enough made believe to satisfy my craving stomach; where I have swallowed "savoury cutlet", "vegetable steak", and I know not what windy insufficiencies tricked up under specious names. One place do I recall where you had a complete dinner for sixpence—I dare not try to remember the items. But well indeed do I see the faces of the guests—poor clerks and shopboys, bloodless girls and women of many sorts—all endeavouring to find a relish in lentil soup and haricot something-or-other. It was a grotesquely heart-breaking sight.
>
> I hate with a bitter hatred the names of lentils and haricots—those pretentious cheats of the appetite, those tabulated humbugs, those certificated aridities calling themselves human food! An ounce of either, we are told, is equivalent to—how many pounds?—of the best rumpsteak. There are not many ounces of common sense in the brain of him who proves it, or of him who believes it. In some countries, this stuff is eaten by choice; in England only dire need can compel its consumption. Lentils and haricots are not merely insipid; frequent use of them causes something like nausea. Preach and tabulate as you will, the English palate—which is the supreme judge — rejects this farinaceous makeshift. Even as it rejects vegetables without the natural concomitant of meat; as it rejects oatmeal-porridge and griddle-cakes for a mid-day meal; as it rejects lemonade and ginger-ale as substitutes for honest beer.
>
> What is the intellectual and moral state of that man who really believes that chemical analysis can be an equivalent for natural gusto?—I will get more nourishment out of an inch of right Cambridge sausage; aye, out of a couple of ounces of honest tripe; than can be yielded me by half a hundredweight of the best lentils ever grown.

One may just suspect the posturer in the turn of some of these sentences, but the suspicion would be worse than unkind—it would be wholly wrongheaded. We have here our man to the the life, speaking from knowledge, as we do again when Gissing is carried on by a natural progression from meat and vegetables to butter. "The deterioration of English butter", he says, "is one of the worst signs of the moral state of our people." He intends no paradox of the kind the solid Englishman likes well enough to make him tolerant of wild Irishmen. He speaks in earnest, and the declaration on butter introduces a reasonable argument—reasonable and urbanely phrased, but expressive of deep feeling.

This comes close to the heart of what I am concerned to bring out. The Gissing revealed in *The Private Papers of Henry Ryecroft* is a man who has achieved peace by the acquisition of steady common sense, which does not stifle, but merely directs and controls, a native sturdy independence and a native fund of deep and true feeling. He is cultivated—that is, he has absorbed much of the past, and has discovered himself and enriched himself—and chastened himself too—by his response to "the best that has been thought and said in the world". Thus he has bound himself to the larger or spiritual life of the race by the only social ties a man can accept with the certainty that they will never gall or strangle him, but will infallibly bring him to the fullest humanity of which he is capable. And though cultivation has detached him from the merely contemporary and the merely immediate interests which tyrannically imprison most of us, it has not robbed him of sympathy. Mr. Swinnerton would have been correct and, indeed, a servant of light, had he said that Gissing "did not love his fellow men" *indiscriminately*. He was certainly not long guilty of the self-deception required in order to conjure up a false sympathy for "man-in-general", and his unqualified love and allegiance were in fact reserved for qualities, for spiritual values, as they are now often called; but this only means that the sympathy he did feel for actual fellow men was honest and true—and for such sympathy Gissing had a real though not unlimited capacity. It was, however, not because of deficient sympathy, but directly because he could and did "look life squarely in the eyes", and was not blinded by a sham abstract "sympathy" or by prejudice, that he finally turned away from humanitarianism

44

and socialism. The Gissing of *The Private Papers* has long been convinced that men are not by nature equal, that some are better than others, that there is a natural aristocracy of intellect and feeling and character, and that the aristocratic principle is the only one which conforms to the unalterable given facts of life. And consistently with this he has also faced and accepted the fact that real education can be received only by a few in each generation, and that the mass of half-educated or quarter-educated people in our time constitute simply an unprecedented menace to civilization, their wind-blown self-sufficiency coming back upon them as well as upon all of us as a cruelly ironic curse.

Such conclusions, of course, cannot be expected to become popular, but neither they nor any others set forth in *The Private Papers* are indicative of the "abysmal selfishness" of which Gissing has sometimes been accused. The following passage fairly, and plainly enough, elucidates the critical attitude which can be mistaken for a selfish or anti-social position by the hasty and prejudiced reader:

> All men my brothers? Nay, thank Heaven that they are not! I will do harm, if I can help it, to no one; I will wish good to all; but I will make no pretence of personal kindliness where, in the nature of things, it cannot be felt. I have grimaced a smile and pattered unmeaning words to many a person whom I despised or from whom in heart I shrank; I did so because I had not courage to do otherwise. For a man conscious of such weakness, the best is to live apart from the world. Brave Samuel Johnson! One such truth-teller is worth all the moralists and preachers who ever laboured to humanize mankind. Had *he* withdrawn into solitude, it would have been a national loss. Every one of his blunt, fearless words had more value than a whole evangel on the lips of a timidly good man. It is thus that the commonalty, however well clad, should be treated. So seldom does the fool or the ruffian in broadcloth hear his just designation; so seldom is the man found who has the right to address him by it. By the bandying of insults we profit nothing; there can be no useful rebuke which is exposed to a *tu quoque*. But, as the world is, an honest and wise man should have a rough tongue.

Obviously, though none of us may *like* to think so, this is realistic common sense; and it is noteworthy that as Gissing

45

attained it he was drawn to Dr. Johnson;—with whom, for instance, he shared a just appreciation of the material basis upon which everything good in life rests. In true Johnsonian vein he says:

> You tell me that money cannot buy the things most precious. Your commonplace proves that you have never known the lack of it. When I think of all the sorrow and the barrenness that has been wrought in my life by want of a few more pounds per annum than I was able to earn, I stand aghast at money's significance ... I think it would scarce be an exaggeration to say that there is no moral good which has not to be paid for in coin of the realm.

And despite Gissing's lack of Dr. Johnson's burly assertiveness in social intercourse, his inward perceptions were straight and true, and exhibit in the realm of thought a right Johnsonian sensibleness, enlightened and heartening. Two more examples must be quoted. Gissing, or Ryecroft, tells how he stood one day watching harvesters at work, until "a foolish envy took hold upon him". He continues:

> There comes the old idle dream: balance of mind and body, perfect physical health combined with the fulness of intellectual vigour. Why should I not be there in the harvest field, if so it pleased me, yet none the less live for thought? Many a theorist holds the thing possible, and looks to its coming in a better time. If so, two changes must needs come before it: there will no longer exist a profession of literature, and all but the whole of every library will be destroyed...
>
> It is idle to talk to us of "the Greeks". The people we mean when so naming them were a few little communities, living under very peculiar conditions, and endowed by Nature with the most exceptional characteristics. The sporadic civilization which we are too much in the habit of regarding as if it had been no less stable than brilliant, was a succession of the briefest splendours, gleaming here and there from the coasts of the Aegean to those of the western Mediterranean. Our heritage of Greek literature and art is priceless; the example of Greek life possesses for us not the slightest value. The Greeks had nothing alien to study—not even a foreign or dead language. They read hardly at all, preferring to listen. They were a slave-holding people, much given to social amusement, and hardly knowing what we call industry. Their ignorance was vast, their wisdom a grace of the gods. Together with their fair intelligence, they had grave moral weaknesses. If

we could see and speak with an average Athenian of the Periclean age, he would cause no little disappointment—there would be so much of the barbarian in him, and at the same time of the decadent, than we had anticipated. More than possible even his physique would be a disillusion. Leave him in that old world, which is precious to the imagination of a few, but to the business and bosoms of the modern multitude irrelevant as Memphis or Babylon.

No unlearned man, no man who was not himself a classical scholar of parts, could have written these words; but equally no man could have reached these conclusions who was intimidated by learning or by convention. And the same independent clear-sightedness is the distinguishing characteristic of the following remarkable passage:

I wonder whether there are many men who have the same feeling with regard to "science" as I have? It is something more than a prejudice; often it takes the form of a dread, almost a terror. Even those branches of science which are concerned with things that interest me—which deal with plants and animals and the heaven of stars—even these I cannot contemplate without uneasiness, a spiritual disaffection; new discoveries, new theories, however they engage my intelligence, soon weary me, and in some way depress. When it comes to other kinds of science—the science blatant and ubiquitous—the science by which men become millionaires—I am possessed with an angry hostility, a resentful apprehension. This was born in me, no doubt; I cannot trace it to circumstances of my life, or to any particular moment of my mental growth. My boyish delight in Carlyle doubtless nourished the temper, but did not Carlyle so delight me because of what was already in my mind: I remember, as a lad, looking at complicated machinery with a shrinking uneasiness which, of course, I did not understand; I remember the sort of disturbed contemptuousness with which, in my time of "examinations", I dismissed "science papers". It is intelligible enough to me now, that unformed fear: the ground of my antipathy has grown clear enough. I hate and fear "science" because of my conviction that, for long to come if not for ever, it will be the remorseless enemy of mankind. I see it destroying all simplicity and gentleness of life, all the beauty of the world; I see it restoring barbarism under a mask of civilization; I see it darkening men's minds and hardening their hearts; I see it bringing a time of vast conflicts, which will pale into insignificance "the thousand wars of old", and, as likely as not, will whelm all the laborious advances of mankind in blood-drenched chaos.

Yet to rail against it is as idle as to quarrel with any other force of nature. For myself, I can hold apart, and see as little as possible of the thing I deemed accursed. But I think of some who are dear to me, whose life will be lived in the hard and fierce new age . . . Oh, the generous hopes and aspirations of forty years ago! Science, then, was seen as the deliverer; only a few could prophesy its tyranny, could foresee that it would revive old evils and trample on the promises of its beginnings. This is the course of things; we must accept it. But it is some comfort to me that I—poor little mortal—have had no part in bringing the tyrant to his throne.

Though all the evidence, it seems to me, is on his side, here no less than when he is speaking of "the Greeks", Gissing is so far from the irrational hopefulness which we cherish in ourselves and encourage in each other that I should have hesitated to quote this passage had it not been too characteristic to be omitted. I fancy, however, there are more now than there were thirty years ago, or even ten years ago, who can discern a sober wisdom in Gissing's hostility to applied science; and I am encouraged in this supposition by a pronouncement of Dr. Bronislaw Malinowski, the great anthropologist of the University of London, which accidentally comes to hand as I write, and shows that in his own way Dr. Malinowski has reached very much the same conclusions as Gissing.[2] Thus it appears likely that here as elsewhere in his reflections Gissing expresses, not indeed the common sense of his generation, nor of ours, but the larger, deeper common sense of the race, the true consensus of enlightened, chastened minds on the question of human living.

And though the picture I have drawn is a bare enough outline, and nothing less than a reading of *The Private Papers* can suffice to bring out the full quality of the mature man so pleasingly revealed there, still, what has been quoted and said should enable us to recognize his unpretentiousness, his cultivation and restrained independence and sanity, his disillusioned yet not unfeeling serenity, his sweetness, and his firm simple decency. I particularly want to draw attention to the fact that he is thoughtful without being a "Thinker", or a "Constructive Thinker". One friendly critic of Gissing has lamented this intellectual modesty, apparently believing it a pity that he failed to elaborate some new kind of philosophy, like George Meredith for example,[3] but it seems to me that this contentment with the role of the critical observer and inquirer is one real though negative reason for his vitality. Despite all of Meredith's brilliance and fire, which Gissing did not share, his novels are fading away into the realm of the "historically important" document at the same time that Gissing's are coming to be thought more interesting and valuable because of their continuing pertinence. Meredith's so-called philosophy already seems shallow, a construction hurriedly run up to meet very temporary conditions and now gaping at every joint. At a forced auction I believe it would scarcely bring a tenth of its one-time valuation. Gissing, saved by modesty and scepticism from a life-long effort to build a new house of cards, went more quietly and simply about the artist's true business, with the consequence that though his novels too are historical documents, they have their basis in life rather than in problems, and so have a perennial human interest transcending the local and passing conditions and questions to which they owe their outer form.

So also in *The Private Papers* Gissing gives us beyond all else the revelation of a man. And this is why the book must be read through for its full effect, even though it abounds in quotable passages which are also very revealing—such as the one where Ryecroft is made to tell how it was a mental peculiarity of his as a school-boy "that at five o'clock in the morning he could apply himself with gusto to mathematics, a subject loathsome to him at any other time of the day". Mr. Frank Swinnerton, perversely looking at the *Papers* as a collection of "thoughts", is puzzled when he considers the love readers have felt for the book, very like the love felt for Boswell's *Life of Johnson*. He complains that the thoughts are really not striking or extraordinary, and that if the book as a whole were not primarily the disclosure of a personality some parts of it would not, as he rather mysteriously says, have any value at all.

I am anxious not to attribute to Gissing any value that he does not have, and I will agree to the justice of Mr. Swinnerton's depreciation whenever it is shown that unpretentious right-mindedness and decency and balance, organically united in a very human figure, are banal and insignificant. There is, to be sure, a rather widespread opinion, not at all peculiar to our time, though taken more seriously than in some former ages, that only human freaks of one kind or another can have absorbing interest for us, so that the study of literature and of life tends to be accommodated to the level of those who find their pleasure and appropriate instruction in the side-shows of a circus. Gissing is not for them. The true meaning of Gissing's life and work, and the secret of his vitality, can be summed up by saying that he himself did indeed begin life as a species of freak, determined to go his own way in his own fashion and act out his sacred impulses regardless of the world, but that he was capable of learning from experience, and thus very gradually re-formed himself, until at last he attained the full, sane humanity reflected in *The Private Papers of Henry Ryecroft.* Hence it is that in order to understand Gissing it is not alone necessary to know this book, but necessary equally to contemplate it in the light of its far background. Gissing's wavering but real growth or development, indeed, from his young manhood to the time of the *The Private Papers,* is that which gives the book its deepest significance—and that which makes Gissing himself a subject of continuing vital interest.

3

At the age of sixteen Gissing entered Owens College, at Manchester. His father had died several years earlier; his mother never exerted any positive influence over him; and his brothers and sisters were all younger than he, and not blessed or cursed with any unusual talent or intellectual capacity. His family lived in the village of Wakefield, where he was born and where he early gave evidence of extraordinary love of knowledge and of extraordinary powers for its acquisition. At school he won practically every prize which he tried to obtain, and in 1872 he was ranked first amongst all those in England who took the Oxford local examinations. After his father's death, the boy's only hope of completing his education rested upon his ability to win a scholarship, but this he easily did, though it only took him to Manchester—not Oxford, not Cambridge.

Under all the circumstances it would have been surprising had Gissing's career at school not raised up in him a little youthful arrogance, and there is in fact evidence to show that from boyhood on he was very conscious of his intellectual superiority. This consciousness was practically his only resource, moreover when he was set free to shift for himself in Manchester. The college was young, had almost no corporate social existence, and made no demands upon its members outside of the lecture-room and the examination-hall. And Gissing had no friends, no one whom he knew even slightly, either in the city or at the college, when he went there. He stood up well for a time under loneliness, without guidance, spurred only by the desire to excel, and at the close of his first year carried off many prizes as usual. There is a picture of him doing so in the opening chapter of one of the best and strongest of his novels, *Born in Exile*. But in the following year he fell in with a young prostitute who had a pathetic story, doubtless true enough, and who succeeded in awakening his compassion. Becoming attached to her, he determined to rescue her from her shameful life and to bring her back to self-respect. He even determined to marry her when this result should be accomplished.

In forming these designs Gissing was merely acting on a conviction which was in the nineteenth century and is today very commonly entertained—a conviction in terms of which much of our social activity is now organized, and one upon whose basis many think they see a new and better religion arising, to replace the shabby and childish Christianity of the ages of pre-scientific faith. For the youthful Gissing assumed that all his poor girl lacked was the mere opportunity to be decent and good. Give her but a chance, he said, and she will go straight. Her fault is not her own;—it has been imposed upon her by a cruel and heartless society. Set right the social order, and you will discover this girl, or any other like her, blossoming as a pure and tender flower. The one crucial difference between the Gissing of this time and the average humanitarian was that he was not able to believe something without acting upon it immediately, consistently, and whole-heartedly. From what is

51

known of the matter one cannot tell how far the girl fell in with Gissing's designs for her or how sincerely. What is certain is that money was required for the endeavour and that Gissing had practically none. We are all familar, alas, with the fanatical humanitarian who is so sure of the excellence and transcendent importance of his ends that he will not hesitate even at murder to achieve them. Two million men and women murdered in Russia testify to the brutal strength of humanitarian zeal when it is once fairly aroused. In Gissing's case, fortunately, murder was not the outcome; but the youth did take to petty thieving from fellow-students, and was caught, convicted, and imprisoned.

When he was released, Gissing could not return to Owens College, nor could he enter any other institution of learning in England. A new start, upon some quite different kind of life, had to be made. Several citizens of Manchester, recognizing that this was no ordinary case of dishonesty, attempted to give aid, and after the failure of one experiment raised money with which Gissing sailed for the United States, to try his fortune in wholly new surroundings. That experiment also failed, and after twelve months he returned to England, sought out the girl who had altered the whole course and character of his life, and married her. It was under these circumstances that he came to London, in October, 1877, to take up the career of a novelist and man of letters. He had no money, no connections, and no capacity for bringing himself into notice. He had written some short stories or sketches in the United States, and had sold them; but they showed no promise, and it is exceedingly difficult to believe that even a very youthful writer could have thought them a foundation for a literary career. His motives for marrying were doubtless mixed, but certainly amongst them was a persisting confidence that he could "save" the girl, and, no less certainly, an acute need for intimate and sympathetic companionship—a need which Gissing felt with unabated insistence as long as he lived, without being able to satisfy it save during the last six years of his existence. For this first marriage turned out exactly as any one could have told him it was most likely to, and as one or two people did try to tell him it would. Within a year or thereabouts his wife became a confirmed drunkard, and when she wanted money that Gissing

52

did not have she returned to her former trade. She thus left Gissing several times and came back repentant when she was reduced to the point of not even having a place in which to sleep. By 1880 a definite and final separation had taken place; but Gissing contributed to her support an amount that was large in terms of his income until her death in 1888.

It is unnecessary for my present purpose to tell even briefly the remainder of Gissing's personal history. This is not without poignant interest,[4] but the crucial events just recounted are the foundation of all that Gissing became, and to them we owe his novels. Until the moment when he was placed under arrest he had been headed towards an academic career, which promised to be brilliant but which certainly would have been conventional. What is known about him suggests irresistibly that he never would have realized himself, never would have become thoroughly awake, and able to grow, had he not been plunged into a sea of horrors and left to sink or swim. The notion that the artist is the better for living a Bohemian life is the degeneration of a profound truth. A number of rebellious and visionary young creatures—and with them some others old enough to know better—have been attempting in recent years to persuade us that everybody ought to live creatively, by which they mean in plainer language impulsively, following courses severely reprehended by those who hate anarchy, both within the individual and within society. At the same time a number of critics have been writing as if they believed that a man cannot be a good artist if he does not live the life of a sober and conventional citizen. It would be a blessing if we could all take to heart the story of Jack Sprat and his wife.

It is not that what is one man's meat is another man's poison, cruelly true though this may be on occasion;—it is that some men cannot learn that poison really is poison without tasting it and actually feeling for themselves its deadliness. Most of these unfortunate beings pay the extreme penalty for their headstrong defiance of sense; but to the few who survive humanity owes much, because from amongst them have come great poets, great artists, great teachers. When I speak of Jack Sprat and his wife I do no not mean—need I say?—that we should endeavour to bring in chaos. Well-nigh every good thing which earthly life affords is conditioned by the maintenance of social order and of personal integrity and of respect for tradition. But this itself means that we are not all alike in talent, strength, pertinacity, imagination, feeling, intellect, just as we are not in appearance—else "order" which implies diversity, would be a meaningless word. The conventional and exemplary citizen, backbone of society though he truly is, cannot also be its head and heart; nor can the heart or head be at the same time the backbone. The rebels and critics whom I have cited are both, then, absurdly in the wrong of it. I am here concerned only with "creativeness"; and clearly no social or other changes are ever going to enable us all to live creatively, any more than they are going to make every man a king—nor, *if we had the slightest notion what we were talking of, could we for a moment wish it.* To become creative in any significant way is not a small or light thing. It requires something more and other than freedom to play about irresponsibly in the sunshine. Though we rebel against the structure of life blindly and hotly, we never contrive to escape the fact that for everything we do or become a price is exacted. No man ever born would knowingly choose the life Gissing made for himself—through long years of exile and slow torture—yet nothing less or easier would have brought out all his creative powers or would have truly humanized him.

The consequence of suffering was a group of novels which despite their imperfections and limitations have a fundamental genuineness and strength, a downright honesty and a quality of thoughtfulness, lifting them high above the general run of fiction, and stamping them as the work of a man authentically acquainted, not with the mere surface of existence, but with its inward realities and the dark springs of feeling and of action. It seems to be widely held nowadays that art—and indeed nearly everything else—is a matter of technique. Gissing is only one of many artists who, in painting, in sculpture, in poetry, as well as in fiction prove that honesty and insight and a desperate concern for the first and last things of life is a surer passport to enduring vitality than the most highly finished technique. *The Unclassed, Thyrza, The Nether World, New Grub Street, Born in Exile,* and *The Whirlpool*—to name only the half-dozen which most strongly impress one reader—are extraordinary in their sombre human truth, in their touches of real and human, not fanciful or transcendent beauty, and in their true inwardness. To miss them is to miss the dramatic testimony of a man whose contact with reality was more genuine and important, despite all restrictions, than that of any others in his generation in English-speaking lands.

Gissing's novels, besides, into which he put so much not only of himself but of his own life's story, enable us as we share his experience to follow his growth through experience;—and this in itself, it is time to recognize, is a great thing. When Gissing was swept from his moorings he was only carried out to sea in a more spectacular and painful fashion than large numbers in his day and even larger numbers in ours. Awakened by overt disaster, confronted with the elemental face of things, compelled to struggle for bare existence, Gissing had to re-orient himself. Like the majority of us, he was dazzled by "the progress of knowledge" and outraged by the progress of industrialism. Perhaps inevitably, he was first impelled to eat more of the cake that had poisoned him. He listened eagerly to the plausible arguments of those who looked forward and proposed to assist in, and hasten, the processes of evolutionary change. He cast off whatever shreds of Christianity there may have been clinging to him and became a militant "rationalist"; became also a positivist, a socialist, a communist, while "his heart burned with wrath and envy of 'the privileged classes'". He mounted the soap-box and harangued the mob while at the same time he put his shoulder to the less exciting and more difficult task of trying to educate working people and of forming amongst them organized centres of class-consciousness and of resistance to oppression. This occurred when he was about twenty—and the consequence was that as he actually tested the dogma of natural goodness and the religion of humanity and the doctrinaire social and educational programmes then more novel but still today prevalent, as he actually lived and worked with and for those who were to possess the earth in the coming better time, he was gradually constrained, to his own dismay, in his own despite, to turn off, first from one -*ism*, then from another, because fact was too palpably opposed to theory. The instance in his own home was only one instance, but, while it remained unique in painfulness, it came to seem typical of all that met the open eye throughout London, slowly but unescap-ably enforcing the conclusion recorded in *The Private Papers*:

I have known revolt against the privilege of wealth (can I not remember spots in London where I have stood, savage with misery, looking at the prosperous folk who passed?), but I could never feel myself at one with the native poor among whom I dwelt. And for the simplest reason: I came to know them too well. He who cultivates his enthusiasm amid graces and comforts may nourish an illusion with regard to the world below him all his life long, and I do not deny that he may be the better for it; for me, no illusion was possible. I knew the poor, and I knew that their aims were not mine. I knew that the kind of life (such a modest life!) which I should have accepted as little short of the ideal, would have been to them—if they could have been made to understand it—a weariness and a contempt. To ally myself with them against the "upper world" would have been mere dishonesty, or sheer despair. What they at heart desired, was to me barren; what I coveted, was to them for ever incomprehensible.

Gissing at the end was nothing if not modest and unpretentious. As we have seen above from another passage in *The Private Papers*, he hated plutocracy; and it was not for that that he turned from socialism. It was because he could not in honesty avoid the conclusion, as he wrote in a novel published in 1889, "that the differences between the nether and the upper world are purely superficial". He could not remain a humanitarian because he came to know the objects of humanitarianism is founded upon illusion, because he discovered that modern secular communism is identical in spirit and aim and real character with modern plutocracy. He did not, however, turn against socialism with the fury of the renegade; he did not even presume to declare that no good could come from cherishing illusions; he knew only that for himself deception was impossible, and that he must undertake again the search for anchorage.

Where he finally stood, and the personal fulfilment which came with his progress through, and beyond the maze of nineteenth-century knowledge and new constructive thinking, we have seen; and we can see better than he could the meaning of his changes. As he looked back upon it, and thought of all his mistakes and wanderings and discoveries made too late, he was tempted to conclude that his life had been "merely tentative" a broken series of false starts and hopeless new beginnings"—and this accounts for the self-condemnation in the letter from which

I have quoted, wherein gissing anticipated the verdicts of such blind self-absorbed "friends" as Mr. Wells. It is one of the penalties of growth that as a man alters he must look back upon his earlier self and work with distaste, condemning both for their immaturity, their superficiality, or their wrongheadedness. We, however, can easily trace a pattern in Gissing's life and work, and in proportion as we follow it out are bound to recognize there a true development, its stages not arbitrary or unrelated, but leading one to another, and culminating in the formation of a mature and fully humanized man.

Doubtless none of those who are so disastrously busy with their plans for the overturning and remaking of human nature and society could be induced by Gissing's example to pause and open their eyes. In the face of their impregnable self-confidence to hope for that would be a childish folly. Nevertheless, there is today, and there is likely long to be, a challenging pertinence, and a lesson, in the life of this "poor little mortal" for men who do not want to find life a hollow sham or a cruel mockery.

NOTES

1. B. Fehr, *Die Englische Literatur des XIX und XX Jahrbunderts (Berlin, 1923)*.
    Dr. Malinowski is quoted in the Cincinnati Times-Star of 27 April 1935, as saying: "I don't believe in progress! We have over-loaded ourselves with technical inventions—erroneously think that means progress. Many modern moron whirls his car through space at the rate of a hundred miles an hour and foolishly imagines he has progressed vastly over such ancients at Plato and Aristotle—if he ever even heard of them—who could go no more than three miles an hour. Indeed our civilization will have to throw overboard some of its destructive technical inventions or it will annihilate itself."
3. May Yates, *George Gissing, An Appreciation*, p. 101.
4. The whole story is told in the Introduction to my edition of *Workers in the Dawn* (2 vols., 1935). Very few, I may add, have ever seen this novel, because it has not hitherto been reprinted and because copies of the original edition are so extremely scarce that one in good condition usually brings a price above $500.00.

57

4

How to Read Gissing

by JOHN HALPERIN*

No English novelist put more of his own life into his novels than George Gissing. To read his books without a detailed knowledge of his biography is to read blind-folded. The critic who attempts to deal with Gissing's fiction phenomenologically of from a narrow structuralist approach has little chance of understanding him. Gissing's work offers an unrivalled challenge to biographical criticism to show what it can do.

No more than a sketch of the life can be given here. Gissing's father was a pharmacist, an amateur botanist, and a dabbler in local politics—an intelligent and sensitive man. Gissing's mother was apparently less sympathetic—religious, narrow, unimaginative. Born in Yorkshire in 1857 into this lower-middle-class family (two brothers, two sisters), the future novelist received a classical education at a local school and at fourteen was awarded a scholarship at Owens College, Manchester. After doing brilliantly there and passing the matriculation examination for London University, Gissing was expelled from the Manchester school for stealing money. He had become romantically entangled with a young prostitute, Nell Harrison, and wanted to help her. He was sent to prison at hard labour for a month and of course had to abandon any idea of a university career. After this he spent a year in America teaching, writing, and nearly starving to death. When he returned to London he took up with Nell again, and married her in 1879—despite the fact that he had probably contracted syphilis from her several years earlier. Gissing lived with Nell

* "How to Read Gissing" by John Halperin: reprinted from *English Literature in Transition*, 1977, pp. 188-98, by permission of the editors.

until 1883, by which time her promiscuity and her alcoholism with its attendant incipient lunacy had destroyed his small stock of peace of mind. He left her, and lived alone for the next seven years (Nell died in 1888). By the late 1880s Gissing's writings were beginning to earn enough for travel abroad; still, he never realized enough from them—even during his years of comparative comfort in the mid-1890s—to relax for long, or to stop working for more than a few weeks at a time. In 1890 in a fit of loneliness he picked up Edith Underwood, a working-class girl, married her in 1891, and lived with her until 1897, when her bouts of violent temper and her inability to run their household exasperated him beyond recall. Once again, he left his wife. The marriage had produced two sons. One lived with Gissing's sisters in Yorkshire; the other stayed with Edith until 1902, when she was institutionalized (he then joined his brother; Edith died in 1917). Gissing spent his last years in France in a common-law union (somewhat less stormy than the others) with Gabrielle Fleury, the French translator of *New Grub Street,* and seeking a climate congenial to his weakening lungs. He died in 1903, of pneumonia, in France. Gabrielle lived on until 1954. The elder Gissing son died in World War I, the younger lived until 1975.

These bare facts, plus some knowledge of the man's neurotic temperament, are indispensable to the would-be Gissing critic.

A fatalist who in his twenties looked in his handkerchief when he coughed and at thirty was sure he was about to die, Gissing believed that peace and happiness eluded most men, and certainly had eluded him. A compulsive reader, a student of languages, an accomplished classicist, the fastidious, hypersensitive Gissing craved order and solitude yet frequently complained of loneliness. Simultaneously a recluse and a claustrophobe, he rarely introduced his friends to one another and thought the custom of people living in close proximity to each other was monstrous. A hypochondriac, he had all kinds of dietary fetishes (he thought Gabrielle's mother was systematically trying to kill him with her cooking), worried constantly about the weather, and never rested. He tried riding a bicycle for exercise but found it made him too nervous. When his friend H.G. Wells wrote that "the *genre* of Gissing's novels is nervous exhaustion",[1] Wells was referring to the atmosphere in which the novels were written as well as to the books themselves. Despite his tendency to self-pity, Gissing could be cheerful; he had a rather grim sense of humour, liked to talk, was attractive to women, and in some moods hated to be by himself. He was probably what modern psychology would term a manic-depressive. He threw out half of what he wrote; everything he completed was abandoned and begun several times before it was finished.

And what did this great neurotic write about? Almost exclusively, the twenty-two novels and a cluster of stories are about *exogamy,* marriage outside one's class. Under this single umbrella may be gathered his three most obsessive concerns: money, sex, and class. For Gissing, one's financial and social position determine one's class—not necessarily one's "natural" class but rather the class in which one happens to find oneself—and this in turn controls one's choice of a partner in marriage and the probable results of that choice. Marriages within a single class are more likely to succeed than exogamous ones, which are doomed by the novelist—a conservative intellectual who twice married culturally deprived women—to failure. Since the exogamous marriage occurs most often in Gissing's novels, we are treated, in them, to a series of domestic disasters.

Gissing wrote about such things both because they obsessed him and because they happened to him. His novels, written directly from life, are without exception parts of a spiritual autobiography and extracts from the facts of his life. But this is not all. Sometimes Gissing took a cue from the characters he created and imitated them in his own life. Oscar Wilde's argument that life imitates art rather than vice versa is convincingly dramatized in the life of his contemporary Gissing, who was prone to act out roles and situations he had dreamed up as a novelist years before. He wrote of himself in his books, creating art out of life; and then, sometimes, he turned art back into life by re-enacting in his "real" life inventions from his fiction. Take the story of Arthur Peachey in *In the Year of Jubilee* (1894). In the mid-1890s Gissing, like his character, was afraid to come home at night for fear of what he might find when he got there. Edith's misery as a housekeeper and mother was often translated into sudden fits of violence upon their small son. Edith is Ada Peachey in the novel. Arthur finally has enough. Taking advantage of his wife's absence from home one day, he moves out, takes the boy to his sister in the country, and then sets up as a bachelor in another part of London without telling his wife his new address. Three years *after* thepublication of *In the Year of Jubilee* Gissing did exactly these things. In him real life and imaginative life often interacted and at times became inseparable.

"You will not find my true self in these books," Gissing wrote to Gabrielle in 1898. This was during their courtship, however, and Gissing was afraid that a careful reading of his bleak early novels might scare her away from intimacy with him. More candid is a passage he wrote at the end of *The Private Papers of Henry Ryecroft* (1901-2), in some ways his most autobiographical work: "May I look back on life as a long task duly completed—a piece of biography," muses Ryecroft, like Gissing a writer, "faulty enough, but good as I could make it—and, with no thought but one of contentment, welcome the repose to follow when I have breathed 'Finis'". Gissing saw life—at least his own—as "a piece of biography", and this is how he wrote about it. The idea of the novelist as biographer is of course a common one in the nineteenth century, reaching a kind of apotheosis in the novels of Henry James; but in works by Jane Austen, George Eliot, Trollope and many of their contemporaries, the novelist-biographer relates the "true history" of a fictional personage—plausible, but not really real.

Gissing knew what he was doing and was aware of the dangers—Kingcote in *Isabel Clarendon* (1886), for example, warns another character against being, in a story, "too subjective. It reads too much like a personal experience, which the writer is not far enough away from to describe with regard to artistic proportion." But his own feelings and experiences were too rich a mine to ignore. In a letter to his friend Eduard Bertz in 1891, Gissing says that "The artist makes all. . . miseries subserve his higher ends." Writing to his sister Ellen in the same year, he declares: "miseries are useful in giving a peculiar originality to my work." Waymark, the novelist-hero of *The Unclassed* (1884), puts it this way: "Art, nowadays, must be the mouthpiece of misery, for misery is the key-note of modern-life." Gissing was certainly miserable enough of the time to take this path in his books toward "modern life". The misery of modern life as it appeared to Gissing is articulated with equal pungency both in the fiction[2] and in the more private writings:[3]

History is a nightmare of horrors. (*Ryecroft Papers*).

Life is a terrific struggle. (*Born in Exile*, 1892)

Life was a perpetual struggle, and, let dreamers say what they might, would never be anything else. (*Our Friend the Charlatan*, 1901)

How . . . in the names of sense and mercy, is mankind content to live in such a world as this? (*Will Warburton*, 1905)

The thing is, to get through life with as little suffering as possible. (*The Whirlpool*, 1897)

The world's about as bad a place as one could well imagine, at all events for most people who live in it. (*A Life's Morning*, 1888)

I dread the sight of strangers . . . For me there have always been two entities—myself and the world, and the normal relation between these two has been hostile. (*Ryecroft Papers*)

Is there any mortal in the whole world upon whom I could. . . . . depend for sympathetic understanding? . . . To every man it is decreed: thou shall live alone. (*Ryecroft Papers*)

I must not pretend to care very much about the future of the human race; come what may, folly and misery are sure to be the prevalent features of life. (Gissings to Wells in 1901)

If I could some day tell you the story of my life, you would see in it a dreary sort of tragedy, but it would explain *me*. (Gissing to Gabrielle in 1899)

Keep apart, keep apart, and preserve one's soul alive—that is the teaching for the day. It is ill to have been born in these times, but one can make a world within a world. (Gissing to his brother Algernon in 1885)

The "world within a world" is the world of fiction—but less an escape from the "outer" world than a reflection or extension of it. Like his character Emma in *Demos* (1886), Gissing tells stories with unhappy endings for a very good reason:

> Emma saw too deeply into the facts of life, and was herself too sad to cease her music on a merry chord; and . . . it was half a matter of principle with her to make the little ones thoughtful and sympathetic; she believed they would grow up kinder and more self-reliant if they were in the habit of thinking that we are ever dependent on each other for solace and strengthening under the burden of life.

James, who met Gissing several times in the 1890s, said later that Gissing was a man "quite particularly marked out for what is called in his and my profession an unhappy ending". "Gissing loves unhappiness", V.S. Pritchett has written.[4] "To understand him one must look first and last at his personal life, for he was, excessively, a personal writer." At what point Gissing's fiction becomes "excessively" personal is open to question. Gissing's books are gloomy because he was a gloomy man. It is probably true, as C.P. Snow has written (in *Homecomings*), that "In your deepest relations, there is only one test of what you profoundly want: it consists of what happens to you". What Gissing consciously wanted and what happened to him were not always the same things, though his judgment does not take into account the possibly self-destructive urges of the subconscious man; but to see this, or anything else of importance about him, we must look to the novels, which symbolize his "deepest relations". They reveal Gissing even more clearly than do his letters, in which there is some measure of self-dramatisation. Fiction, after all, is likely to be much more revealing than conscious autobiography, in which there is often some holding back. An autobiography can distort; facts can be realigned. But "fiction never lies; it reveals the writer totally", says V.S. Naipaul. One of Gissing's great contemporaries knew this well enough. "A writer of imaginative prose . . . stands confessed in his work", Conrad wrote in *A Personal Record* (1912). "He stands there, the only reality in an invented world, among imaginary things, happenings, and people. Writing about them, he is only writing about himself. . . . Indeed, everyone who puts pen to paper . . . can speak of nothing else."

One of the things we are likely to remember most vividly about Gissing's characters is their savage moodiness, what today we would call their unfortunate *nerves*. These are at the root of their unhappiness, their "misery". Kingcote in *Isabel Clarendon*, one of Gissing's most autobiographical protagonists, confesses: "I do not know what it is to have the same mind for two days together. My enthusiasm of to-day will be my disgust of tomorrow. I am always seeking, never finding . . . My moods are tyrannous; my moods make my whole life. Others have intellect; I have only temperament." Gissing could be virtually clinical in his observation of himself: indeed, what Kingcote says here is an illuminating and at least as accurate as anything about Gissing written later by such intimate acquaintances as Wells or Morley Roberts or his sister Ellen. The narrator of *Isabel Clarendon* goes on: "Kingcote had often asked himself what was the purpose of his life—here it had declared itself at length. This was the fulfilment of his destiny—to suffer. He was born with the nerves of suffering developed as they are in few men." It is with this sort of equipment that the protagonists of Gissing's novels attempt to face the difficulties of modern life. "It has pleased Heaven to give me a splenetic disposition, and some day . . . I shall find the tongue," says Waymark, another alter-ego, in *The Unclassed*, Gissing's second published novel. Lionel Tarrant in *In the Year of Jubilee* published ten years later, "finds his tongue" as a "splenetic" journalist writing cutting articles. Like Kingcote, Widdowson in *The Odd Women* (1893) is unable to "take things the simple way that comes natural to other men" but instead is "always . . . full of worrying problems." Ellen Gissing wrote after her brother's death that his apparent "gloom" could be explained in part by his desire to suffer "rather than bring suffering upon others": fair enough, but no man *willingly* suffers all of the time, even to provide himself with material for fiction. Gissing's general pessimism grew out of his vision of himself, or perhaps rather the place he occupied, in the world he lived in—a vision shaped partly by his reading of Schopenhauer, which provided him with a justification, a philosophic defense, and a powerful rationalization of his condition and the conclusions it drove him to. But partly too, primarily in fact, his view of things was a result less of his reading than of his temperament. That he could not, in any case, visualize *himself* apart from questions of sex, money, and class explains their confluence and their constant presence in his thought, and thus in his fiction. These obsessions bring us back to the exogamy theme.

We must consider first Gissing's problem with women, for there is not doubt that he had a problem. In *The Born Exile* Gillian Tindall points out that Gissing made the mistake of marrying beneath him not once but twice, that both Nell and Edith eventually went mad, and that Gabrielle too had her eccentricities. Are we to believe, asks Tindall, "that this was a total coincidence?. . . . Anyone may marry one highly neurotic woman by accident . . . but to embark on something like a marriage with three argues a particular emotional taste." One explanation of the "odd" women in Gissing's life is that he was constantly haunted by his own misfortunes—especially his prison term and his venereal disease—to the extent that he thought himself unfit to live with a woman of refinement. He may, of course, have preferred lower-class women, though what we know of him makes this unlikely; certainly for a novelist he was an astonishingly poor judge of character. Perhaps he was a masochist. Undoubtedly he had what Tindall calls "fatal sexual susceptibilities". The narrator of "A Lodger in Maze Pond" (1894) admits: "I am a fool about women . . . It's sheer sentimentality, I suppose. I can't be friendly with a woman without drifting into mawkish tenderness . . . There's that need in me—the incessant hunger for a woman's sympathy and affection." And he adds, significantly: "I find it an impossible thing to imagine myself offering marriage—making love—to a girl such as those I meet in the big houses." A few years earlier Gissing wrote to Bertz: "there's no *real* hope of my ever marrying any one of a better mind, no *real* hope whatever!" Between wives at the time, he added: "This solitude is killing me. I can't endure it any longer. In London I must resume my old search for some decent working-girl who will come and live with me. I am too poor to marry an equal, and cannot live alone" (shortly after writing this he picked up Edith). One can accept the latter clause of Gissing's final sentence without necessarily believing the former. Too poor? Or too insecure, too guilt-ridden? Gissing's abhorrence of the working classes, expressed throughout his life in different ways, suggests that he did not seek out lower-class women because he preferred the class to which they belonged. He may have had a need to depreciate women—or, rather, to feel assured that, in his wife's eyes, he was a superior being. More to the point, he saw himself as unworthy of any "respectable" woman, and this is largely because his idealized woman was the ideal of a snob. His novels tend naively to equate good manners and breeding with moral worthiness, while the poor and uneducated are usually rated at face value. Everywhere he speaks of the desirability of marrying a "respectable" woman. "To me that has always been the one, the only thing in the end worth living for," says Kingcote in *Isabel Clarendon*. Gissing's more sympathetic heroes tend to be men of lower-class, or lower-middle-class, origin who hope to find a "respectable" woman to marry, yet are often deterred by poverty or by some past crime—real or imagined—brought on by poverty or their origin will ultimately alienate the chosen lady. Some take the plunge and then discover that poverty can destroy any affection, that no love can survive the corrosive effects of empty pockets, or that social inequality can eventually make enemies of husband and wife. Some simply give up and marry, disastrously, beneath them. "The love of a true woman is always precious. That of a woman who is one's intellectual equal (or superior) is a blessing beyond any other known to this life of ours," Gissing wrote to Gabrielle in 1898. He told Bertz in the same year that his literary efforts had been undertaken primarily to achieve " that much greater thing, the love of the ideal woman." As late as *Will Warburton*—written when Gissing had been living with Gabrielle for several years—the hero is a man who "had never yet succeeded in persuading himself that any girl. . . . was at all likely to conceive the idea of devoting herself to his happiness." Usually, in Gissing's view, such aspirations ended in disillusionment—either because the pursuit of financial independence was too degrading or the woman herself was seen ultimately to be unworthy. "To win the love of a woman," says Peak in *Born in Exile*, "I have had to behave like the grovelling villain who has no desire but to fill his pockets." "Marriage rarely means happiness," *The Whirlpool* announces; better to remain a boy, it suggests, than grow into a man and face "the curse of sex". In 1893, in the third year of his marriage to Edith, Gissing complained to Bertz: "more than half the misery of life is due to the ignorance and childishness of women. The average woman pretty closely resembles, in all intellectual considerations, the average male *idiot*—I speak medically . . . I am driven frantic by the crass imbecility of the typical woman." *The Whirlpool*, written in the year in which Gissing left Edith, refers to "that crime of crimes, the begetting of children by a worthless mother". "The woman who may with safety be taken in marriage by a poor man given to intellectual pursuits is . . . extremely difficult of discovery", says the narrator of *Isabel Clarendon*. In this way sex, money, and class become one subject in Gissing's fiction, the subject of marriage.

Perhaps more than any other, the question of *class* obsessed Gissing. Throughout his work is an "exile" theme; it always concerns men whose intellect and education make their most natural associates the intellectual elite of the middle class but whose poverty dooms them forever to familiarity with the lower strata. "It is my fate in life to be known by the first-class people and to associate with the second class—or even the third and fourth. It will always be so," Gissing wrote to Bertz in 1890 (he may have felt a little differently a decade later). Waymark in *The Unclassed*, Kirkwood in *The Nether World* (1889), and Peak in *Born in Exile* are only three examples of the typical Gissing hero—by origin a member of the working class but with feelings, susceptibilites, goals, and an education which make him unhappy in this lower rank of life (perhaps the most spectacularly *déclassé* of the protagonists is Will Warburton, an upper-middle-class businessman forced by economic reversals to become a grocer). Peak blames "fortune" for having "decreed his birth in a social sphere where he must ever be an alien". He tells Sidwell Warricombe (the idealized woman in *Born in Exile*): "My life has been one of slavery and exile . . . from the day of my birth." As he attempts to achieve social respectability Peak is driven continually to worry about leftover "marks of the ignoble world from which he sprang" such as any "defect of pronunciation" or "awkwardness of utterance". The *genre* of nervous exhaustion, indeed. Gissing's hatred of his essentially working-class origin was always a source of secret guilt. "I cannot look at the *hands* of a toiling man or woman without feeling deeply wretched. To compare my own with them, shames me", he wrote in his Commonplace

Book. The heroine of *Thyrza* (1887) tells Egremont, the Gissing persona of that novel: "You have talked to me of your natural nearness to people of the working class, and I firmly believe that you are further from them . . . than many a man who counts kindred among the peerage. You have a great deal of spiritual pride." Such pride was in itself a source of satisfaction to Gissing, though he sometimes felt guilty about it. Like Egremont, Gissing at one time wanted to open free schools for working-class men and women in which lectures on literature and philosophy would be offered—in part an impulse of genuine concern, surely, but just as surely a demonstration of his own superiority to and distance from those for whom such education was considered necessary. "Social grades were an inseparable part of his view of life", it is said of the hero of *Will Warburton*. Pritchett is surely right to call Gissing "the most class-conscious of our novelists".

But it is as impossible to consider women apart from questions of class in Gissing's work as it is to consider questions of class apart from those of money. Always memorable in these books is the collision between the man of intellect, usually educated sufficiently to be disappointed by the limitations fate has placed on him, and the grinding necessity of his earning an income large enough to satisfy his own yearnings or his family's wants—both of which are always more than minimal. Here the civilizing effects of education are seen to be in fact pernicious, tantalizing without being able to assuage. No other novelist has written so movingly of the pulverizing effects of poverty on the sentient spirit and of the ways in which human feelings can be degraded by economic pressures. Gissing, according to Roberts, described his fictional heroes as belonging generally to "a class of young men distinctive of our time—well-educated, fairly bred, but without money". It is the focus on the individual confronted by economic circumstances beyond his control that gives such power to Gissing's best novels. Among dozens of passages a reader of Gissing could think of in this connection, two may be quoted here. The first is from *New Grub Street* (1891), where the novelist Reardon tells his wife:

> I have no sympathy with the stoical point of view; between wealth and poverty is just the difference between the whole man

and the maimed. . . Can I think of a single subject in all the sphere of my experience without the consciousness that I see it through the medium of poverty? I have no enjoyment which isn't tainted by that thought, and I can suffer no pain which it doesn't increase. The curse of poverty is to the modern world what that of slavery was to the ancient. . . You remember the line of Homer I have often quoted about the demoralising effect of enslavement; poverty degrades in the same way.

"Poverty degrades"—this is a radical theme in Gissing. The other passage is from *The Crown of Life* (1900): here the writer speaks directly to the reader:

The brute force of money; the negation of the individual—these, the evils of our time, found their supreme expression in the city of London. Here was opulence at home and superb; here must poverty lurk and shrink, feeling itself alive only on sufferance; the din of highway and byway was a voice of blustering conquest, bidding the weaker stand aside or be crushed. Here no man was a human being, but each merely a portion of an inconceivably complicated mechanism.

"Poverty," says Gissing in *The Nether World*, "makes a crime of every indulgence." It was always with the novelist both a haunting memory of the past and an obsessive fear for the future. "I can't be at my ease in society, simply because I can't do justice to myself", says Jasper Milvain early on in *New Grub Street*. "Want of money makes me the inferior of people I talk with, though I might be superior to them in most things." There is a long procession of such men through Gissing's novels. Hilliard in *Eve's Ransom* (1895) wonders how "people feel who are quite sure they can never want as long as they live." Such people seem to him to inhabit another universe. Kirkwood in *The Nether World* understands instinctively "how men have gone mad under the pressure of household cares". For Tarrant in *In the Year of Jubilee*—who, like Gissing himself, was always sure he was going to be run over in the street by an omnibus— the "social question" simply resolves itself into "man. . . . asking himself how he is going to keep body and soul together." There is a spiritual problem, however: "No matter how pure the motive, a man cannot devote his days to squeezing out pecuniary profits without some moral detriment (*Will Warburton*). The artist's case is even more difficult; more than

other men, he should try to be impervious to material needs—
and yet without freedom from such anxieties, in Gissing's view,
he cannot work at all. "Art, you know, is only contemptible
when it supports the artist", snarls the bitter hero of *A Life's
Morning*. Yet "the educated man who marries on less than a
thousand is either mad or a criminal" (*The Whirlpool*).

What is a man to do, then? Work until he dies. This is what
Gissing had to do. By the 1890s he was often ranked with
Meredith and Hardy among the leading novelists of the time,
yet his books never made much money. He always had to work
hard; a constant source of anxiety was the knowledge that if he
were ever unable to work for any significant length of time he
would soon be utterly penurious. And so he spent his final years
seeking healthy climates, knowing that for him work would
always be a necessity. We have seen why Gissing thought of
himself as having been born in exile; the novel of that name, like
In the Year of Jubilee, contains a curious bit of uncanny
prevision—in this case the story of a man who driven by social
and financial pressures out of his native England, dies in self-
imposed exile. Gissing died in the Basque Pyrenees, a novel
(*Veranilda*) unfinished, Wells and Gabrielle haggling at his
bedside over the respective merits of English and French
nursing methods.

As early as 1897 Wells wrote that Gissing "has been learning
life and his art simultaneously". More recently Jacob Korg has
said that "the rivalry between legitimate narrative interests and
didactic autobiographical motivations creates a sense of strain
in Most of Gissing's novels."[5] Indeed, this "rivalry" frames and
informs almost all of Gissing's fiction. Critics have often
recognized something like this, but what little there is in print
about Gissing has not gone nearly far enough. Some of the most
interesting work has been done by Korg and Tindall. Factually
reliable, Korg's excellent biography, *George Gissing* (1963), is
not, and does not purport to be, a detailed critical study of the
fiction. Tindall's assessment, long on psychoanalysis, is short
on common sense—a perceptive reader of Gissing's mind,
Tindall is an imperceptive reader of his books. Recent studies of
Gissing by Adrian Poole (a very unscholarly monograph) and
Michael Collie (a biography full of inaccuracies) do not fill the
void. Pierre Coustillas's brilliant scholarship has been channeled

so far into bringing most Gissing material to light and reconstructing the novelist's life into what undoubtedly will be an important biography when it appears several years hence. So: some of the major tasks of Gissing criticism remain to be done. To recognize that Gissing's life and work are inseparable, in some ways symbiotic, is important, but it is not to investigate this relationship or show how it exists. The fiction and the biographical materials must be encountered, and assessed, together. Before anything else, we must learn how to read Gissing.

NOTES

1. Quoted by Gillian Tindall in *The Born Exile: George Gissing* (London, 1974), p. 247.
2. There is still no collected standard edition of Gissing's work, though the Harvester Press is bringing out a new critical edition a volume at a time. Whenever possible, my quotations here are taken from the first English edition of the novels, usually the most reliable; but as is often the case in Gissing studies, these were not always readily available to me—so in some instances I have used other editions.
3. Here and throughout, references to Gissing's letters are to the following volumes: *The Letters of George Gissing to Members of His Family*, ed. by Algernon and Ellen Gissing (London, 1927): *The Letters of George Gissing to Eduard Bertz, 1887-1903*, ed. by Arthur C. Young (New Brunswick, NJ, 1961); *George Gissing and H.G. Wells: Their Friendship and Correspondence*, ed. by Royal A. Gettman (Urbana, Ill., 1961); and *The Letters of George Gissing to Gabrielle Fleury*, ed. by Pierre Coustillas (New York, 1964).
4. See his introduction to the Signet edition of *The Private Papers of Henry Ryecroft* (New York, 1961).
5. See Korg's introduction to his edition of *George Gissing's Commonplace Book* (New York, 1962).

71

5

The Exile of
George Gissing

by MORLEY ROBERTS*

It is a favourite idea of mine that most strong writers are men of one theme only, and that in such a singleness lies the secret of their effectiveness and strength. However this may be, and I am not concerned to support the thesis, it appears certain that this in no small measure was the case with George Gissing. He had one dominant, one overpowering idea, and it returns with almost as sure a certainty as the *leitmotif* of one of Wagner's operas. This master idea is one which colours his life and his work; it becomes at last more than idea, it is an atmosphere. There is no escape from it, either for him or those who read his books, though I have no doubt that he himself was only rarely conscious of its eternal presence.

In any writer, in any artist, there must be some such element beyond the worker's knowledge, and I do not think it can be denied that the task of the critic is to seek out and thus lay bare the true origin of the artistic work with which he has to deal. If on analysis the subject thus yields up its secret a great light is cast upon the man and the books on which he spent his life. Without any such clue all study is as barren as science without the fertile aid of hypothesis. That there is such a clue to George Gissing may, I think, be shown without any great subtlety or without torturing the facts. I write, not as one wholly without the illumination which comes from personal knowledge, but as

* Reprinted from *The Albany Magazine* (London), Christmas 1904, by Morley Roberts, pp. 24-31.

72

one who knew no little of his writings and the way they were written, or one who was a witness of many of his struggles, as one who was acquainted with his life, his character, his sufferings, and his aspirations.

There are those, I know, who profess that it is not seemly to indulge at this hour in anything like comparative criticism of his books. Nevertheless it appears to me that no critical canon can be of any value whatsoever which does not lead to such judgments while it makes clear the reasons on which those judgments should be founded. I think that the time must come when not a little of his work will be esteemed of little value. From this I doubt if he would have himself dissented with any particular reluctance. I find some of his books great in the abiding sense of the word; some of them though not so worthy, which are true and bitter studies of observation; some of them infinitely valuable to the student of letters and humanity as suggesting what he might have been had the gods smiled upon him; and some that I cannot read in spite of the ability which is apparent in all he did.

The books of his that will live are those written with his blood and on fire with the flame in which he burned. They speak directly and with the bitterest power of what he suffered in the life to which few were admitted, and of the anguish he endured while he made his name. In these books there is nothing strained, nothing false, nothing invented, nothing that does not ring as true as real life itself to those who are yet in the fire and to those who are beyond it. In *Born in Exile* he spoke in a parable of a man born out of place, of a man who loved all beautiful things with a passion that the brutalities in which he found himself could not destroy. Gissing was this man; he had been born outside of the paradise of ease and beauty. He was in every fibre a hedonist. He adored the beauty of women, the scent of flowers, the breath of the wind which blows in the lovely places of the earth, the savours of a feast, the bouquet of wines—in a word, all those things for which the intellectually sensuous must inevitably yearn. The idea of the exile was ever in his mind, and when he wrote this book he wrote under a thin cover of himself. There are times when any sacrifice seemed justifiable if only one could compass that which meant ease of living and the free play of the mind with his chosen fellows in an atmosphere which was not foul with the gross poverty he knew so well. In another book he wrote with the most concentrated bitterness, "Put money in thy purse, and again put money in thy purse, for, as the world is ordered, to lack current coin is to lack the privileges of humanity, and indigence is the death of the soul." This is why such books as *Born in Exile* and *New Grub Street* stand out in the ranks of his work like pillars; for this reason they will endure when much that is good will be as dust. The enduring qualities in all great things is not the artistry, as the foolish do most vainly imagine, but their essential truth; not their power of words, but the fire and the blood behind the words. In these books there is more of him in his essence than there is even in "Ryecroft"; for, though he told some truth there, it was only a truth that was by the way and not the truth that was in him. It is the shadow of the man but not the man himself, though great parts of it bleed and are most affecting.

Of his other books I confess to the greatest love for *By the Ionian Sea*. This was, again, the man on one of his most characteristic sides. I have sometimes thought that he would have been at his very best if he had been born in the time when the Renaissance was in its flower. The fathers of the Renaissance re-discovered Rome and Athens, and so did he. Nothing can persuade me, if this had been his fate, that his name now would have have been as sacred to all who love letters, because they helped to free the human mind, as those of Petrarch and his glorious band of fellows. It was this quality of his which gave him his contempt for the obscurantist theologian. I see him in my mind treating, with the irony which was his favourite weapon, some relic of the Dark Ages. He gloried strangely in the Greece he knew at last, for he saw it as it had been, not as it is with the modern Greek shrieking in the market-place. His historic imagination was of that high order which permits a man to live in history, even though he fail in writing it. When he saw the Acropolis he saw it before the Turks had stabled their horses there, and before worse Vandals than the Turks had brought into exile the marbles of Phidias. He loved the roar and the fume of Rome, and in Italy he saw that land which gave the world Dante and Boccaccio, and was yet peopled in the south with such as they had known. The sight of the oxen made him literally shout for joy. Such oxen Hannibal had seen, such had drawn the vintaged Falernian to the house of Horace. When once had had visited the imperial city and Italy he came back to another world as he read Virgil, for at last he could stage the epic and the Bucolics in his own renewed and most fertile mind. To hear him mouth the mighty verse of the great Greeks, who are dead and yet alive, was always wonderful, but after he had seen Piraeus and the peopled mountains of Greece, Homer was something other than he had been, and the language of Aeschylus and Sophocles took on it new glories and clothed itself in still more wondrous music. A hundred choruses he knew by heart, and he declaimed them with his wild hair flung back and with his eyes shining, as if the old tragedians, standing in the golden sun of Hellas, were there to hear him, an alien yet no alien, use the tongue they gave its chiefest glory to for ever. If he had not been born in exile he might have done such things as would have cast greyer shade the great grey works he wrought in this cold England. How strange a thing it was that his colour sense lay utterly dormant till he went to the land of his dreams! In his rooms in the old days there was not a spot of any colour, all in it was grey, or black and white. He had engravings, but not even one painting, and he glorified in the accomplishment of his desire to see the ancient world.

If one has to think of his work, then, as of one born in exile, it is natural enough that the critical faculty cannot be satisfied with all he did. Those books of his that stand in the second rank of his achievement are such as *Thyrza, The Nether World*, and *In the Year of Jubilee*. To speak thus of them is not, I affirm, in any way to disparage them. In my mind there are few serious novels of the few last years of the century that are worthy to compare with them in force and in utter sincerity of workmanship. They must fall short of his greater and more personal books, but that they rise as high as they do is a powerful reinforcement of the thesis I propound concerning all his work. In these he no longer treats directly of himself, and yet where does the beauty of them lie but in the beauty of one in alien surroundings? And where does the bitterness of his exiled mind show itself if not in the fierce, ironic things that in like case he would have found intolerable? The motto on the title page of *The Nether World* is full corroboration of this: *"La peinture d'un fumier peut être justifiée pourvu qu'il y pousse une belle fleur: sans cela, le fumier n'est que repoussant.* " This theme may not be, and indeed is not, the chief theme of all his books, but in one form or another it can be discovered, for it was vital to the man, the outcome of his life, of his history, and at last of his second nature. In the possession of one such dominating motive he was like most great artists. It is no derogation, but rather praise, to show that in this he was of their brotherhood. By his own pain he taught, and he had suffered greatly. There is much of his own work but that must be classed not so much by its merit as by the absence of that observation which filled such books as I have put in the second rank. If one considers carefully the particular solitariness of his life, and the circumstances of that life itself, it is easy to see that a full knowledge of bitter poverty, and of the very centre of the intellectual slums of such places as the Camberwell of *In the Year of Jubilee*, could hardly be compatible with the knowledge of the middle and the upper middle classes necessary for the success of such books as *The Crown of Life*. As a matter of fact he had not such knowledge: he never had the chance of obtaining it. These books (and here I refer especially to the one last mentioned, *The Whirlpool, Our Friend the Charlatan* and such as *Denzil Quarrier*) are admirably written, they have qualities which might well make a reputation for a lesser man; they are often brilliant in their satire and in their irony, in which only Samuel Butler among his contemporaries excelled him, and yet for all that they lack something which takes them out of the class to which the others certainly belong. In them there is not that same certainty of touch, not that power of full knowledge, not that sureness which comes to a psychologist who has had himself on the dissecting-table and watched his own heart beat and his every nerve quiver. In these he has only too often used that which is second-hand, he has drawn from no fresh spring but from the reservoir of books, in them has resorted to invention and hypothesis and theory. He did not know the upper middle classes, which are as difficult every whit as those beneath them, and take as much time and labour and experience and observation to learn. To those who think it is a hard judgment I say that he never had the opportunity of learning them, and a careful reading of those books will show it. He knew the narrowly religious, the mental barrenness of the poor Dissenters, the people of the slums that he observed so carefully, and many of those on the borders of the Bohemia of which he at last was an initiate, and he was soaked and stained, as he might himself have said, with the dull drabs of the lower middle class that he hated. But of those above he knew little. He only spoke of them because his old material was exhausted, because he strove to put the past behind him when he went to live away from England. And yet had he achieved the freedom of the spirit. Whatever his final success or failure he was, in a literary and artistic sense, still an exile though very near the promised land.

There are many, I know, who will think much of this criticism both ill-founded and unjust. They will deny that he ever did work which can be described by the word that all English artists know only too well. And yet he undoubtedly wrote "potboilers" and knew that he did so. If there are those who doubt it a second reading of *New Grub Street* should convince them of their error. If *Born in Exile* gave us, as I know, the psychologic essence of himself in Godwin Peak, *New Grub Street* gave us the artist striving dreadfully with his surroundings and the horrible discouragements that are the artist's in dire and hopeless poverty, when the absence of joy and success, to say nothing of the food that he needs, renders him doubtful of his powers of continued labour. A thousand times he sat down to work he loathed when he wanted rest to recuperate his worn and tired imagination. Like Reardon, he destroyed whole books; he began and once more began and sat with impotent mind over blank paper that mocked him, or over words, put down in desperation, which had no mates and no meaning. He changed his themes when he should have been able to change the sky that stifled him and the bitter circumstances that had no hope in them. Such a man could not always be at his best. Fate tried him too much for that. He passed much that was not satisfactory to him. He could do no other. He lived in exile and in exile he died.

It is hard to speak without emotion and without pain of *Veranilda*. He believed in it greatly, and yet no more than any writer must while writing. The artist's own illusion of a book's strength and beauty is necessary to any accomplishment. The writer must believe with faith or do nothing. Nevertheless soon it will not be denied that *Veranilda*, with all its colour, its beauty style, its knowledge of the period and its pathetic irony, cannot be reckoned equal to the books that were written with his blood. For want of true understanding of all his work, not a few have failed to see his best. The futile and frigid preface which precedes the published *Veranilda* declares it his greatest achievement, while the perfunctory writer acknowledges his ignorance of much that Gissing wrote and his want of sympathy with not a little. The rejected preface gave a true picture of the man, not unpleasing to those who loved him, but put *Veranilda* above all other work. But *Veranilda* does not possess the true mark which distinguishes the successful historical romance; it has not that powerful conviction, that essential passion of the period, which makes the reader forget his vague knowledge of the time, and makes him say, "This is, this must be, true." When *Veranilda* is compared with the chapters in *By the Ionian Sea*, which treat of Cassiodorus and his country, the merest tyro in criticism cannot fail to see that a personal study by Gissing, a series of travel pictures, would have had the colour, the passion, the individual glory that the book lacks: for his enthusiasm for the past was wonderful, and in this book it would have been out of place and time. It is a splendid failure. The grim necessity which for ever dogged his steps made him cast it in the mould of the romance. But for this he would, I am assured, have given it the world in some such form as *By the Ionian Sea*, and it would have been a possession for ever. His greatest works still remain those he wrote in exile.

6

Gissing's Characterization: Heredity and Environment

by C.J. FRANCIS*

Discussion of Gissing's characterisation is complicated by his frequent, though not total, lack of objectivity: his habit of including sympathetic semi-autobiographical characters, of idealising beautiful women and sensitive scholars, and conversely of expressing loathing of the ugly, vulgar and ignorant. Admittedly, no author, however objective his intention, is likely to see in character other than what he is predisposed to see; the objection to Gissing's subjective attitude is not that it involves a distortion of psychological truth, for that is merely relative, but rather that it leads to inconsistency in the study of motivation. In the same book, some characters may be supplied with the best motives, offered excuses for their conduct; others, less favoured, are presented in worse lights. The author's bias intrudes itself.

Nevertheless, if one attempts to penetrate below this visible bias and ask what Gissing thought constituted character, it appears that he held in common with other Realists a semi-scientific view of psychology, which can be conveniently described under the three headings of heredity, environment and temperament.

He shared in the growing interest of the late nineteenth century novel in the complexity of man's consciousness, for its

* "Gissing's Characterisation: Heredity and Environment" by C.J. Francis: reprinted from the *Literary Half-Yearly*, Vol. III, July 1962, by permission of the editors.

own sake, not only because it led to actions. Of one of his characters, Woodstock in *The Unclassed*, he says,

> I assure you the man is very lifelike; the only thing is that I have ventured to draw him more *faithfully* than any other English novelist would. Human nature is compact of strangely conflicting elements, and I have met men extremely brutal in one way who yet were capable of a good deal of genial feeling in other directions.[1]

He was perfectly aware that character was not so simple a matter as the traditional classical or romantic novelist, and their Victorian descendants, might believe. In such novels, characters were neatly defined, and easily recognised as symbols. Their motives were directly related to their actions and consequently to schemes of virtue and vice, or social morality. But Stendhal in particular and other Realists made clear the new trend, the realisation that the majority of people were complex and did not act from a simple set of rules derived from their character. They realised that people might do the most unexpected and contradictory things; that they were likely to be influenced by their circumstances and surroundings; that they think about their own emotions, consciously attempting to analyse them—but not necessarily acting logically from their conclusions. Even as they came to understand that people were not neatly divided into good and bad, so they realised that they were not even divided into normal and abnormal; moreover, that people's thoughts were not exactly represented by their behaviour.

The psychological theory adduced in explanation was essentially deterministic, as the science and philosophy of the time would lead one to expect. They felt that there was no free will, and actions were wholly determined by motives; consequently, they thought, could all the motives be known, then the action could be accurately forecast. The basic idea was elevated into a thesis by Zola, who placed special emphasis on theories concerning heredity. This last concept, not in itself new (though previously men had thought more of inheritance of physical features than of character), enabled writers to think of men in terms of contemporary evolutionary theory, to see him as one of a species, related to his ancestors, his relatives and the rest of the human race in more than arbitrary ways. Due attention being given to its complications, i.e., that it was no simple rule, that a man was not the sum of the qualities of his parents but a selection of and also of more remote ancestors, it offered an explanation of things otherwise inexplicable: why men should be basically different from one another; why some should be given good characters and some bad, or indeed why they should be born with characters at all.

There is no evidence that Gissing made any close study of heredity, other than a brief mention of "Ribot's *Hérédité Psycologique*" as the reading matter of a "progressive" woman[2] which appears to have no special significance. Morley Roberts says that he made no study of technical psychology at all[3] which seems probable. Nevertheless, as May Yates points out, he was sufficiently concerned with it to take care over making his characters consistent with their parentage, when it is mentioned.[4] She instances five characters. Thyrza, the girl of low social class who is yet refined, is provided by the author with a mother of some refinement as an explanation. (I would add that Arthur Golding, the artistic slum child in *Workers in the Dawn*, in similar fashion is made the son of a gentleman.)

Clara Hewett, in *The Nether World*, is as impatient of parental authority and poverty as her father is rebellious against social conditions. Godwin Peak's father, like his son, is of low birth but with strong impulses towards culture; he has a violent personal pride and perversity that recurs in his son's reasons for leaving the University and his awkwardness in accepting help (*Born in Exile*). Reardon's father betrayed the same lack of pertinacity as his son (*New Grub Street*).

Richard Dagworthy of *A Life's Morning* is an especially good example. He

> represented an intermediate stage of development between the hard-headed operative who conquers wealth, and his descendant who shall know what use to make of it.[5]

His father had been a cunning, industrious and boorish business man; Richard "had doubtless advanced the character of the stock, and possessed many tastes of which the old man had no notion."[6] The tragedy of his existence is the clash between ambitions towards gentility and refinement, aroused in him by the circumstance of inheriting wealth and consequently being brought up to what was materially at least the life of a gentleman; and the ruthlessness, independence and miserliness inherited from his father. Foreign travel was spoiled for him, for instance, because although he had an active curiosity he could not adapt himself to the unfamiliar conditions, presumably because he had not the necessary flexibility of mind; and also because he could not reconcile himself to the expense; "pursuit of money was in him an hereditary instinct".[7]

The result of this clash is that Dagworthy, whose ambition is to marry a woman of refinement, because he feels that this will improve his own way of life, is driven to most ungentlemanly methods to attain his end.

> A mere uneducated Englishman, hitherto balancing always between the calls from above and from below . . . he could make no distinction between the objects which with vehemence, he desired and the spiritual advantage which he felt the attainment would bring to him; and for the simple reason that in this case no such distinction existed. Even as the childhood of civilisation knows virtue only in the form of a concrete deity, so to Dagworthy the higher life of which he was capable took shape as a mortal woman.[8]

The relation in Gissing's mind of hereditary character and the process of human evolution is clear.

Besides these examples given by Yates there are many more. In *The Nether World*, for instance, Jane Snowdon has the gentle nature of her grandfather, though her father is selfish. Sidney Kirkwood's father was, like his son, "an intelligent, warm-hearted man". Clem Peckover's cruelty and cunning is inherited from her mother.

> Who knows [asks Gissing] but this lust of hers for sanguinary domination was the natural enough issue of the brutalising serfdom of her predecessors in the family line of the Peckovers?[9]

It is clear, in fact, that, although Gissing laid no special emphasis on the heredity theory, it lay at the back of his thinking about character. Nor was its importance limited to these studies of descent; it contributed to a special type of consistency in character drawing, typical of Gissing. Not for him are striking changes in character, radical conversions to good or evil such as may be found in romantic novelists of the more facile kind. A slow development and alteration of attitudes can be seen in some characters, but it indicates no basic change; instead it is evidence of wisdom, of the growth in that character of wider and more balanced views of life. This is exactly according to the views of Schopenhauer, whose thinking matched that of the Realists in so many ways; he too believed that a man was born with a fixed inherited character, and that the only development of character was growth of knowledge. In Gissing, such changes are usually changes from bitterness and passion to calm and resignation—so, Gilbert Grail, for instance, who abandons his aspirations as impossible to realise (*Thyrza*). There is one striking change of character, that of Miriam Baske in *The Emancipated*, who from a religious bigot becomes a woman of calm and balanced mind; but this is the result of the growth of knowledge and experience, and the beginning of a study of art, developing potential qualities hitherto cramped by the narrow life of a religious community. The characteristics that were previously developed—sobriety and strength of will—undergo no alteration. Examples of consistency are plentiful. The dissipated Reuben Elgar, for instance, intends to reform himself and make use of his experience:

> All the disorder through which I have gone was a struggle towards self-knowledge and understanding of my time.[10]

—but, perception or no, his basic weakness of will repeatedly prevents him from fulfilling this promise, and he falls again to dissipation.

Widdowson, in *The Odd Women*, has a possessive and jealous character that ruins his relations with his wife. Although he has himself brought about the disaster, he cannot reconcile himself even to believing that the child she bears him is his own, despite his wife's statement on her deathbed. His jealousy is still uncontrollable even when the cause is removed.

Godwin Peak is the opposite case to Elgar; he allows himself to be drawn into a course of deception, but when it is discovered, the strong and independent pride that he inherited from his father recurs; the exposure is almost a relief for him, and he bears it with such dignity as to seem a much better man than he was before.

Pride is the special characteristic also of Rhoda Nunn in *The Odd Women*. It lies behind her efforts towards individual independence of women. Although she does not believe in the forms of marriage, her pride of self in addition to her instinctive upbringing makes her insist that her suitor offer her legal marriage. On reconsideration of her position she decides to uphold the principle she has preached—this also from pride, and causing another clash with her suitor, who has now decided that legal marriage is preferable.

These are examples of situations that frequently occur in Gissing's stories. There is another example that is very convincing: it is the case of the elder Mrs. Mutimer in *Demos*, whose character is one of independence and self-sufficiency. When she is suddenly raised to affluence, she is distressed by the possession of a servant and greatly prefers to continue to do her own work and maintain her own home, to the extent that she does over again the work the servant has done.

This example introduces us to the second division of Realistic psychological theory, the influence of environment; and in doing so presents a problem that must be considered shortly. The interest in environment arises from the deterministic theory that actions follow necessarily on motives; a theory expressed in set terms by Waymark in *The Unclassed*, and more emotionally by Reuben Elgar, who wishes to decline responsibility for his actions:

> I tell you I am conscious of no sins. Of follies, of ignorances, of miseries—as many as you please. And to what account should they all go? Was I so admirably guided in childhood and boyhood that my subsequent life is not to be explained?[11]

Of course determinism is divorced from ordinary morality, as it rejects free will; but we must not be led by Elgar's excusing the satisfaction of impulses, or by Zola and the Naturalistes' emphasis on *"le mécanisme humain"*, into thinking that this doctrine of necessity holds that men act only according to the influences of the moment. Clearly, under "motives" must be included the things of the mind, moral tendencies, prejudices, as well as purely material motives. The psychology of the Realists, I have pointed out, was a complication, not a simplification of character study. Consequently, one cannot illustrate the doctrine of necessity in itself from Gissing's analysis of motives, since those motives will be the same whether such things as moral instincts are regarded as being spiritually imparted or acquired through upbringing. Only, Gissing (while retaining a moral point of reference) tends not to condemn or approve, on the whole, which indicates a feeling that men are not really responsible for their actions.

However, if free choice is denied, it becomes obvious that not only must a preponderance of, for instance, reprehensible motives overcome a commendable motive in one instance, but also that a frequent repetition of the same situation will lead to the commendable motive losing power and significance in the mind of the man concerned. This brings us to the theory of the influence of environment: the circumstances in which a man lives will gradually influence his mental make-up, by constantly presenting to him motives in accord with the necessities of his life. Thus arises the antithesis between the romantic novelist, who believes, for instance, that virtue will always triumph over adversity, and the realist who believes that constant adversity will eventually diminish virtue.

The influence of circumstances is, of course, on the character's outlook; to use Schopenhauer's terms, on the knowing faculty: they do not affect his basic character, which has to do with the will. The examples of consistency of character which I have given are all variations of strength of will and the sense of self-importance.

The influence of environment is the particular aspect of the doctrine of necessity that the Realists set themselves to illustrate. They emphasize the effects of upbringing, as in the case of Reuben Elgar, and his sister Miriam Baske. Moral and religious adherence, it is implied, are not matters of character but only of knowledge, being acquired. So, Miriam becomes a strict religious observer, aided by her character trait of strength of will; in a different environment she loses this outlook, but retains the will. Reuben, in addition to his trait of weak-willed indolence, has strong passions, and the effect of this repressive upbringing is to make him rebel. There is of course no simplification here; the same motives do not produce the same effects, because the characters are different.

More noticeable a subject than the effect of education in Gissing, as in most Realists, is the special effect of poverty (though he showed himself always interested in educational problems). The effects of poverty are his major theme; there is hardly need to demonstrate his studies of ignorance and degradation amongst the lower classes. But it is worth while to observe the case of educated people.

His general theme was the depressing and disabling effect of poverty: of Reardon, he says,

> He was the kind of man who cannot struggle against adverse conditions, but whom prosperity warms to the exercise of his powers.[12]

This situation in various forms arises again and again. Poverty not only cramps the abilities and distracts from concentration, but it develops in a man his less admirable qualities—avarice, cunning, ruthlessness—even though he may have been originally a man of integrity and altruism. This happens to most of the characters in *New Grub Street*. Amy Reardon is unwilling to face poverty; it constricts her love for her husband, and brings her to leave him to his own devices rather than to support him. It makes her think first of money, and only afterwards of artistic integrity and reputation. Her tendency to selfishness and to ungenerous instincts is developed. Reardon too suffers in becoming surly and querulous.

> A little money, and he could have rested secure in her love, for then he would have been able to keep ever before her the best qualities of his heart and brain. Upon him, too, penury had its debasing effect; as he now presented himself he was not a man to be admired or loved.[13]

Alfred Yule's bitterness and vindictiveness is the result of the defeats he has received in the struggle for existence:

> I am all but certain that, if he became rich, he would be a very much kinder man, a better man in every way. It is poverty that has made him worse than he naturally is; it has that effect on almost everybody. Money does harm, too, sometimes. . . . .[14]

Cunning and ruthlessness are more natural to the "villain" of the book, Milvain—but even in him they are emphasized by poverty, as he claims:

> Selfishness—that's one of my faults. . . . If I were rich, I should be a generous and good man; I know I should. So would many another poor fellow whose worst features come out under hardship.[15]

To all these people the same thing is happening: the constant presentation among their motives of the need to get money, at any cost, gradually blunts and renders impotent the motives of generosity, fairness, integrity and the like. It is worth noting that the aspirations of many characters become concentrated on some material object. Peak, like Dagworthy, lets his ambitions turn to acquiring a wife of refinement; Yule lowers his aims from literary success to the editorship of a magazine whence he can avenge himself on his critics.

"Money does harm, too, sometimes. . . ." Though most concerned with poverty, Gissing does not omit to give an example of damage done by wealth. Mutimer, the local leader and socialist speaker in *Demos*, has all the appearance of an honest and sincere man; and, by virtue of these qualities, bids fair to achieve the power and eminence he is led to desire by his character trait of ambition. When he comes into money, the character trait remains, but his behaviour alters in obedience to the change of motives. As he becomes aware of the possibilities that lie before him, he ceases to wish to be a representative of the people and to share their conditions. He retains enough of his social enthusiasm to wish to be a benefactor, and institutes an ideal manufacturing company; but in doing so he shows a growing tendency towards the autocratic methods of the employer. He sets out to acquire a gentlewomen for a wife, and acts unfeelingly towards his former friends.

When a will is discovered that takes away his money, he shows actual dishonesty in attempting to conceal it. Although it is unlikely that he has analysed his own motives, he is betraying that the quest for power is his ruling passion; when success depended on integrity, he found it easy to be honest; now that it depends on the possession of wealth, he is dishonest. As soon as he has lost the money, he takes up again his former character of the honest man. This is a clear case of actions responding directly to motives, given the basic urge to power.

The problem raised by the case of Mrs. Mutimer, his mother, is this: if actions are decided by environment, why does not Mrs. Mutimer adapt herself to the conditions of wealth as her son does? We must begin by admitting that Gissing's irrational prejudice against the lower classes complicates his application of the theory of environment. He is ready enough to show them degraded by poverty; ready to show that such a man as Mutimer would be worse when in possession of wealth; but not to admit that a working-class person has possibilities of improvement. Lady Ogram in *Our Friend the Charlatan* is "an exception to the rule that low-born English girls cannot rise above their native condition".[16] This prejudice has some part in the presentation of Mrs. Mutimer. Mutimer's brother and sister are depraved by wealth, as he is; Mrs. Mutimer is included as another aspect of the thesis that the lower classes cannot rise in the world. Nevertheless, she has the ring of truth; and I think she can reasonably be explained. Her children, whose strength of will, even in Richard, is not strongly developed in the direction of maintenance of principles, react rapidly to the change of circumstance. Mrs. Mutimer's integrity is strong, and her habits of life deeply ingrained with age, so that, within the period of the story during which she is possessed of wealth, she shows no change. It is not that the new circumstances have no effect upon her; they have the effect of making her cling more strongly to her principles. Had Gissing a different purpose in mind, might one reasonably suppose he would have shown us Mrs. Mutimer slowly adapting to the new conditions. His study is usually of the gradual effect of environment; for example, Miriam Baske, equally strong-willed but much younger, does not break away from her narrow intellectual habits until she has for some time been exposed to a freer atmosphere.

Miriam Baske represents the good effects of an improved environment, and reminds us that Gissing does not deal entirely with adverse circumstances. Of course, his essential pessimism predisposed him to descriptions of misery; his own experience gave him special sympathy with the depressed intellectual, so common a figure in realistic novels of the age, and especially amongst Russian realists of the school of Gogol. The feeling of his books is the tortured suffering of Dostoievsky, whom he admired; his characters also were the oppressed and despairing, the "insulted and injured", those who suffered not only material but also social and spiritual harm from their circumstances. Yet he did not intend to convey that the effect of circumstances on character was invariably adverse. He gives full credit to the significance of inborn character (as when the same education has opposite results on Reuben Elgar and Miriam Baske). He does not over-simplify the theory of environmental influences, but he makes full allowance for it in his psychology.

Nor is his handling of the theory so mechanical as this discussion might suggest; he did not write an "experimental novel", but sees his characters as inseparable parts of their environments. The wish expressed by one of Gissing's readers, that he give his characters more money, emphasizes this point.[17] We too sometimes wish that Gissing was a little less oppressively pessimistic; but we realise that not only does the struggle against circumstance form the subject and theme of most of his books, so that without it they would not exist, but also that the characters as they are presented would not exist if they were richer. They would be different men. They might be recognisably similar, but they would have changed in most respects. Gissing does create a few educated protagonists— Mallard (*The Emancipated*), Rolfe (*The Whirlpool*), Langley (*Sleeping Fires*)—who are not poverty-stricken; apart from their individual qualities, they are in general different men from the sufferers. In their personal relationships they are more capable, more balanced; all their faculties and interests are more harmoniously and soundly developed.

NOTES

1. Letter to his brother, 23 June 1884, *Letters of George Gissing to Members of his Family* (London, 1927), p. 141.
2. *The Whirlpool* (London, 1897), chapter III.
3. *The Private Life of Henry Maitland* (London, 1912), p. 193.
4. M. Yates, *George Gissing, an Appreciation* (Manchester, 1922), pp. 60-2.

5. *A Life's Morning* (London, 1888), chapter VIII.
6. *Ibid.*, chapter V.
7. *Ibid.*, chapter VIII.
8. *Ibid.*, chapter XIII.
9. *The Nether World* (London, 1889), chapter I.
10. *The Emancipated* (London, 1890), chapter IV.
11. *Ibid.*
12. *New Grub Street* (London 1891), vol. I, chapter V.
13. *Ibid.*, vol. I, chapter XVII.
14. *Ibid.*, vol. II, chapter II.
15. *Ibid.*, vol. I, chapter VIII.
16. *Our Friend the Charlatan* (London, 1901), chapter VIII.
17. Letter to Morley Roberts, *Bookman* (London), January 1915, p. 123.

7

Gissing's Feminine Portraiture

by PIERRE COUSTILLAS*

It is hardly possible to survey Gissing's ideas on women and femininism without occasionally introducing biographical data. His thought and his marital difficulties are so closely interwoven that one may sometimes need to pause to recollect whether it was Nell or Carrie Mitchell, Edith or Ada Peachey who was concerned in some dimly remembered domestic explosion. Also, the circumstances of Gissing's life influenced the artistic tonality of his work, toward idealism during one stage of his career, toward realism during another.

The correspondence between life and fiction begins with his mother. That he had little affection for her is certain. Indeed, she embodied some of the defects he soon came to abhor in woman. Though the daughter of a well-known Droitwich solicitor, she was poorly educated and showed little interest in the things of the mind. She was content to follow tradition, to be a conscientious Victorian housewife, whose sole ambition was to fulfill her domestic duties, to practise the religion inherited from family tradition or adhered to by a stubborn spirit, and to bring up her children according to rigid moral principles. Mrs. Gissing was helped in her household duties by servants whose activities she supervised with more than ordinary zeal. She was more absorbed by what went on in the kitchen than interested in her husband's scientific occupations. Gissing must assuredly

* "Gissing's Feminine Portraiture" by Pierre Coustillas: reprinted from *English Literature in Transition*, vol. 6, 1963, No. 3, by permission of the author.

have been thinking of his own mother and similar domestic-minded women when he drew Mrs. Mutimer's portrait. The family's sudden accession to prosperity which unexpectedly places her in comfortable circumstances soon gives Mrs. Mutimer reasons to distrust the new order. She pathetically tries to keep her former habits, and like Gissing's mother, she considers domestic duties as the be-all and end-all of married life.

Gissing's two sisters—Margaret and Ellen—were all the more influenced by their mother because Thomas Gissing, the chemist-botanist, died in 1870, when they were still very young children. Until they reached womanhood, Gissing encouraged them to read, to give themselves a liberal education, to break with their austerely provincial ways. He never really prevailed on Margaret to become interested in art. He apparently came nearest to defeating her self-conscious reticence when he persuaded her to accompany him on a tour (Spring, 1889) to the Channel Islands and bathe in the sea. In his diary he complains that to literature she prefers the reading of "some dirty little pietistic work".[1]

But with Ellen he was more successful; she was musical and now and then commented upon her brother's novels. When, in reading *The Emancipated* (1890) it dawned upon her that George might have taken her as a model for the puritanical heroine, Miriam Baske, she inveighed against the spirit of the book and the so-called advanced opinions it expounded. Gissing's reply emphasized the spiritual and moral differences that lay between himself and his family. He did not attack religious faith but formalism and its manifestations. When *Born in Exile* (1892) came out, Margaret was moved to protest: "It is a pity you should write on a subject you so little understand as Christianity.—It would be as reasonable for me to deny the existence of all the beautiful things you have seen and told me of in foreign countries, simply because I have not seen them, as it is for you to deny spiritual things you have never seen or felt, when there are thousands of people who have seen them, and are therefore as certain of them as of their own existence. How anyone can disbelieve the Bible merely because it is not written in the latest scientific language seems remarkable." Gissing copied the passage in his notebook and added: "How impossible to reply to such stuff as this!"[2]

Of his life with Nell (Marianne Helen Harrison), Gissing has left a poignant record in *Workers in the Dawn* (1880) which, with impressive lucidity, foreshadows the outcome of his first marriage. He shows how pity was conducive to love which then degenerated through living together. Though he soon gave up all hope of the purposed reformation of his wife and strikingly conveyed the idea in the novel, he seems to have acknowledged the failure of his idealistic attempt only in his own particular case. Indeed, when in *The Unclassed* (1884) he took up the subject of fallen girls and their possible reclamation, he again gave way to his youthful illusions. Like Nell in real life and Carrie Mitchell in fiction, Ida Starr is a street walker, but unlike them, she succeeds, through sincere love, in resuming the position of an honourable woman and devotes herself to philanthropy. In 1895, when Lawrence and Bullen issued a revised edition of the book, Gissing wrote in a prefatory note: "It will be recognised as the work of a very young man, who dealt in a romantic spirit with the gloomier facts of life."[3] However, in February 1888, after several years of separation marked by increasing debauchery, when Nell died in a Lambeth slum, Gissing felt no remorse. He had done his best to save her from the abyss. More than her weakness, society was to blame and he adopted the only course left to him—artistic revenge—in his next novel. *The Nether World* (1889), the only book he wrote in which the protagonists are exclusively proletarians. He wavered from pity to contempt and disgust and never quite dispelled the ambiguity from his mind.

Similar echoes from his second marriage occur in the novels of the 1890s. The writing of *New Grub Street* (1891) coincides with his courtship of Edith Underwood, the daughter of a plasterer. He first tried to convince her to live with him outside the bonds of marriage—which was a sign of wisdom in one who had so much difficulty in handling the practical side of life. The way out of the difficulty would have been Murger's *grisettes* but they seemed conspicuously absent from Victorian London. At any rate, in *New Grub Street* Gissing covertly examines the pros and cons of the step he is contemplating. After the Manchester episode he thought of himself as an outcast, tacitly accepting society's dictum. True, the prison term he had to serve is not even transposed as it will be in *Born in Exile*. Harold Biffen has not broken his social moorings by offending public morality. Gissing is content with declaring that educated girls never will consent to marry penniless writers, and he is trying to find excuses for his forthcoming marriage with Edith, convincing himself that the impending decision is in very truth the only one open to him. Reardon's apparent luck in marrying a lady dramatically turns against him when creative power deserts him. Alfred Yule's fortune is no better—he has married a working-class girl and, much as Gissing will be, he is ashamed of his wife, whose incorrect speech and vulgar relatives irritate him to frenzy. Gissing's prophetic strains proved of no avail, for he threw himself headlong into trouble when he sent an ultimatum: he hurried the girl into accepting and she did accept. Of what married life became we get a graphic description in *The Year of Jubilee* (1894). Ada Peachey is the embodiment of all the defects he had found in Edith. Besides her domestic inability—a serious deficiency in Gissing's eyes—she only responds to the vulgarity, pretentiousness and ignorance of all about her. Once more, he prophetically apprehends the future. Ada, like Edith, exasperates her husband by her unruly and violent behaviour, her quarrels with the servants. Both Gissing and Peachey are driven from their homes.

Then Peachey is reconciled with Ada, who feigns remorse at her past conduct, and her second child is born of this capitulation. Gissing's second son was born of some such matrimonial patching-up, and Gissing himself was to flee from his wife for a few months in the spring of 1897 before he left her for good when a new attempt at cohabiting had failed, as it had in the Peachey *ménage*.

Just as *Workers in the Dawn* and *In the Year of Jubilee* retraced or adumbrated the difficulties and disaster of his first two marriages, *The Crown of Life* (1899) was inspired by his love for Gabrielle Fleury whom he met for the first time at the home of H.G. Wells when she came to England to talk over with him the translation of *New Grub Street* into French. The Swift-like tone of the anti-imperialistic satire alternates with the rather languid romantic passages describing Piers Otway's passion. Gissing planned to write another book, in the style of *Ryecroft* (1903), to glorify his love for his French wife, but unfortunately the project was not even sketched, since *Veranilda* (1905), on which he was working in December 1903, was not completed before his death. From his encounter with Nell at Manchester to his exile in France, Gissing had gone the long way from idealism to the ideal. He had vainly tried to reform a prostitute who might have dragged him into debauchery with her, had he not, by sheer force of will, resisted her; then his union with Edith Underwood, given his temper and ideas, was doomed to failure; at length he had found the ideal wife who, besides her native French, could speak English, German and Italian, and play the piano with distinction. She was greatly interested in literature and a frequenter of Parisian literary circles. Because she increased his European interests and culture, his last books have a wider breadth of thought.

2

I have already shown, in broad outline, how Gissing's circumstances influenced the content of his novels and particularly his portraits of women who mirror his mother and sisters, Nell Harrison, Edith Underwood, and Gabrielle Fleury. A closer inspection of the novels reveals Gissing's desperately clinging to an idealistic view in his artistic rendition of his circumstances. His efforts to maintain the idealistic vision, however, finally give way to a realistic tonality.

In *Workers in the Dawn*, and even in earlier short stories,[4] the idealist-realist dichotomy is evident. Carrie Mitchell and Helen Norman are the opposites to which Arthur Golding succumbs. Whereas his union with Carrie is depicted with unrelenting fidelity to facts, his platonic love for Helen, in which one discerns the author's thirst for womanly refinement, is described in ethereal strains. Gissing's power will rarely, if ever, reach such poignant intensity as in those scenes which express Arthur's heart torment. Symbolically torn between his two irreconcilable ideals—social reform and a whole-hearted devotion to art—Golding is the first full-length figure of man as a victim of love.

In *The Unclassed*, Julian Casti allows himself to be blackmailed into marrying his cousin Harriet Smales who soon

95

becomes a dauntless shrew. His friend Osmond Waymark, whilst comparing married life to slavery, indulges in idealistic dreams. The woman he dreams of is she who, though involved in the basest acts of life, keeps her soul undefiled. Although in 1884, Gissing had outlived his enthusiasm for Comtist positivism and his allegiance to Frederic Harrison's ideas, he would not admit that his marriage with Nell was doomed to failure; he was still enough of an idealist to have his prostitute heroine Ida Starr redeemed by love.

His idealism changed in quality when, through the Harrisons, he became acquainted with the Gaussen family at Broughton Hall in Oxfordshire. Mrs. Gaussen was an aristocratic lady of good education with flagrant social prejudices, much at ease in society. Gissing's visits to Broughton, at a time when he had lost faith in radicalism and was taking a well-defined artistic stand, led him to a phase of rather priggish conservatism noted for markedly idealised creations. Looking upon a class of society of which he had hitherto no direct experience, he is in a position to renew his fictional material and his critical attitude to working-class aspirations and socialism with the palpable result that the conservative press gives some eulogistic reviews of his next novels. At that stage in his career social conservatism goes hand in hand with an idealistic impulse bitterly critical of progress. It is remarkable that each of his next three books—*Isabel Clarendon* (1886), *A Life's Morning* (1888) and *Demos* (1886)—has an idealised heroine. Indeed, the model for the first of them was no other than Mrs. Gaussen herself. Bernard Kingcote, to whom Gissing gave his own retiring habits and intellectual tastes, is faced with the question that was increasingly to obsess his creator—can a poor, though well-educated, sensitive young man marry a lady like Isabel Clarendon? Kingcote's answer is a masochistic "No". He thinks he has no right to condemn her to poverty, to desecrate his ideal. Just as Gissing thought that his disgrace in Manchester debarred him from marrying an educated girl after Nell's death, Kingcote considers his family duties—i.e. material aid to his widowed sister—as an indomitable obstacle to his marriage with Isabel. Gissing lends his heroine the wordly manners he had found so attractive in the lady of Broughton Hall; she is feminine without frivolity and moves with disarmingly natural grace among her admiring acquaintances. Her education partakes more of society savoir-faire than of intellectual distinction—she prefers the reading of magazines to that of Sir Thomas Browne. But Kingcote the plebeian is too deeply in love to realize that she fails to satisfy hiw views on culture. Throughout the novel Gissing is arguing with himself and draws his best inspiration from self-inflicted mental agony. In *Workers in the Dawn*, a sort of social *fatum* hung over the novel; in *Isabel Clarendon*, it is psychic as well as social.

Better than *A Life's Morning*—a poor key to Gissing's intentions since he had to tag a happy ending on to it to please James Payn—*Demos* shows how painfully class-conscious he had become by the end of 1885. Adela Mutimer looks at her husband's face, while he is asleep in the train to London: "Their life of union was a mockery: their marrried intimacy was an unnatural horror. He was not of her class, not of her world; only by violent wrenching of the laws of nature had they come together. . . To be her equal this man must be born again."[5] Yet, contemptuous as Gissing had grown of working-class manners and ignorance, he could be moved to pity by the hardships of the poor, as can be seen in his treatment of Mutimer's discarded *fiancée*, Emma Vine. In *Thyrza* (1887), he gives us his most highly idealized female character of working-class origin, a *belle fleur* grown in dingy surroundings. No doubt self-pity once more serves as the mainspring of inspiration, as Gissing identifies himself with the suffering, wronged élite of the people.

3

The shock caused by his first wife's death in in February 1888 brought an abrupt change in the tone of his next novel—*The Nether World* in which he reverted to the dominantly realistic accents of *Workers in the Dawn*, though with a more skilful pen. It contains a masterly gallery of female portraits whose realism is a worthy tribute to Nell's memory—a victim of poverty and drink. There we find Clara Hewett with her face disfigured by vitriol, Pennyloaf Candy with her loafer of a husband and Clem Peckover, that panther of a woman. With these personages, Gissing reaches to the depths of cruelty and vulgarity, and physical and moral degradation. *The Nether World* marks a break in his life as much as in his works. Never more will he return to the painting of the poorer classes; the curtain falls on the world of prostitutes, of work-girls sweated to exhaustion, of sly-tongued, filthy landladies. When he heard in Paris from Smith, Elder that they would pay a hundred fifty pounds for his novel he went to Italy and from then on his subjects, taken from the middle classes, are elaborated with greater detachment.

The Emancipated, for example, is instinct with a subtle humour which mainly affects the two heroines, Miriam Baske and Cecily Doran. *The Odd Women* (1893), his most telling contribution to the feminist cause, centres rather on the material, as opposed to the spiritual, side of woman's emancipation; it happily combines irony and realism within a fairly didactic framework. In the most serious novels of the early nineties, *New Grub Street, Born in Exile* and *Eve's Ransom* (1895) in particular, the harsh tone precisely coincides with the time of Gissing's second plunge into self-defeat. The subject became too painful to him and he abandoned introspection.[6] He now studies his heroines from the outside. However, while Louise Derrick and Polly Sparkes strike us as clever attempts at bright, attractive characterization, they cannot rival their predessors of the 1880s. It was not until Gissing wrote his critical study of Dickens, in Siena, far from his termagant wife, that he unsealed the torrent of his wrath. He had chosen liberty and freely gave voice to his bitterness in describing Dickens's carping women. "Their characteristic is acidity of temper and boundless licence of querulous or insulting talk. The real business of their lives is to make all about them as uncomfortable as they can. Invariably they are unintelligent and untaught; very often they are flagrantly imbecile . . . It is difficult to believe that death can stifle them; one imagines them upon the threshold of some other world, sounding confusion among unhappy spirits who hoped to have found peace."[7]

After his return to milder realism, Gissing, under the influence of Gabrielle Fleury, reverted to idealism in *The Crown of Life*. Irene Derwent reminds one of Isabel Clarendon, with less loveliness and greater perfection. She also embodies Gissing's romantic idealism which, kept down by his intellectual desire to paint life realistically, nevertheless crops up now and then under various forms such as the Manchester episode and the flight to France in May 1899 on the one hand, such literary creations as Helen Norman, the lady of Knightswell or Stella Westlake, on the other. Gissing, like his hero Piers Otway, had achieved the ideal which Arthur Golding had failed to embrace.

4

Although his portraits of women and the tonality of his work were influenced by the circumstances of his life and although he was sensitive to the social currents of his time, Gissing is no theoretician or reformer; he has no remedy to propose for the evils he depicts. He is primarily a novelist and an artist who represents contemporary English life as he sees it with his inborn and acquired pessimism; though his novels may appear to the casual readers as novels with a purpose, they have no other ambition than to present a disillusioned view of late nineteenth-century English society and they may be called, as one critic said, "thesis novels without a thesis".[8] Gissing was irritated by Edith Sichel's "Two Philanthropic Novelists",[9] because he was compared to Besant, whom he held in scant esteem as an inartistic writer of rose-water fiction and above all because he was labelled a philanthropist, a notion particularly unpalatable to him when he was writing *The Nether World*, inspired by Nell's death. With the possible exception of *The Odd Women*, Gissing's own opinions are either confirmed by repetition or expressed in his letters and diary.

A Victorian in spite of himself, Gissing implies by repetition that he would have woman be the mistress as well as the ornament of the household; on the purely domestic side of her functions the two extremes to be avoided are overbearingness and fussiness; material domestic life should be considered as a means and not an end, carried on in order and silence. Of the household virtues of English housewives, he entertains deep-rooted suspicion. At the lower end of the scale we have Mrs. Pettindund in *Workers in the Dawn*, a monster of inefficiency and intemperance, and Carrie Mitchell, who like Alice Madden in *The Odd Women* drinks in secret and her real home is the street and the public house. At their best his housewives, though they

99

exert themselves with competence and zeal, render their very best qualities a burden to their family because of their stubbornness and unadaptability. They are all too apt to be frightened by change, typically, Mrs. Hood in *A Life's Morning* and Mrs. Mutimer in *Demos*. Their capacity lies in their plodding unintelligent conscientiousness. At the other extreme is Alma Rolfe in *The Whirlpool* (1897) who, by giving way to the maelstrom of London society, loses all interest in, and feeling, for family life and undutifully neglects her own child.[10]

Gissing's feelings towards woman lie between two poles: on the one hand, intense admiration of sensual origin, an irrepressible aspiration for absolute happiness, for example, Arthur Golding's love for Helen Norman in *Workers in the Dawn* and Piers Otway's for Irene Derwent in *The Crown of Life*; on the other hand, cynicism and a hardly contained craving for violence which find full expression for the first time in *New Grub Street*. It is doubtless significant that in the first two books he does not allow love to bear the test of marriage. Helen Norman requites Arthur's love but the latter's legal link with Carrie frustrates all hope of a life in common for the two lovers; Helen dies of consumption in France and Arthur commits suicide by plunging into Niagara Falls. In *The Crown of Life*, the action comes to an end with the prospect of marriage, precisely Gissing's own situation in January 1899, when he penned the last chapter of the novel. Rarely does he show married life in anything but a bitterly critical light; in fact even Gabrielle Fleury herself before the mysterious "ceremony", held at Rouen on 7 May 1899, was disturbed by reading his novels. He admitted that he had darkened his pictures out of bitterness, but his nature had a strong pessimistic bent as she was to realize.

In all but his very last novels Gissing delights in analyzing the causes of failure, the process of degradation, with a keenness all the greater as he draws his inspiration from his own life, or what he clear-sightedly senses it will be, a delectation of intellectual, even cerebral, order with a masochistic strain. Marriage, he repeatedly says in various ways, is the most ironical of counter-apotheoses: at first blindfolded by passion, man very soon perceives the devastating extent of his illusions. Carrie Mitchell is lifted out of vice temporarily, only to fall back deeper into disorderliness, dragging her husband down for a while. In *The Emancipated*, after her elopement, Cecily discovers that she has married a debauched blackguard. Wedlock is padlock, an unnatural institution from which Gissing himself twice vainly tried to find a release. In the cage of connubial life, debarred from liberty by law and moral canons, Gissing contemplates resort to violence against his irascible wife. The idea comes up for the first time in *New Grub Street* in the famous scene between Amy and Reardon. In his next novel, *Born in Exile*, Earwaker tells Peak how he came to renounce the idea of marriage: "I foresaw a terrible possibility—that I might beat my wife."[11] The suggestion occurred to him at the time when he courted Edith Underwood—an action he was later to call criminal—but it is to his critical study of Dickens that we must turn to appreciate his obsession.[12] To the problem of life in common, Gissing has Tarrant offer a radical solution in *The Year of Jubilee:* let husband and wife live under separate roofs and only meet when the spirit moves them. Thus the main cause of the deterioration of love, of conjugal misunderstanding—namely live together under legal compulsion—will disappear. Nancy submissively accepts Tarrant's condition because she knows her love will live through it. In the same novel, he seeks the cause of woman's demon-like behaviour. In the lower middle class, he has Peachey say that the fiasco of married life is due to her lack of a proper sense of responsibility, to her failure to fulfil her household duties, to her dislike of humble pleasures, to her having no religion. And, indeed, Gissing's novels are teeming with domestically incapable women dreaming of vulgar entertainments. No moral system has any hold over them. Though many have not yet altogether abandoned religious practice, church-going has become to them a mere perfunctory habit devoid of any spiritual commitment, a mere sign of that outward respectability they set so much store by.

Socially, woman represents a conservative force, at least mainly among the people—a part of the population still barely affected by the essential emancipating factor—education. The example of Mrs. Alfred Yule reminds us of Mrs. Mutimer and Mrs. Hood. The three of them are distrustful of changes, whether for better or for worse; their sturdy attachment to routine will replace reflection, which, in their own particular case, may well be more of a good point than a defect. False emancipation Gissing repeatedly satirizes. In *Demos*, Alice Mutimer whose sudden fortune has awakened the bad instincts that lay dormant in her, is duped by a bigamous adventurer and dishonoured. In *The Town Traveller* (1898), Gissing paints the character of Polly Sparkes with humour but her native vulgarity and racy impertinence leave us in no doubt as to what married life will be with her nincompoop of a husband. In both cases the social emancipation of woman assumes a purely negative form: rejection of marital authority, complacency in domestic quarrels, a resolve to enjoy one's rights without recognition of one's duties.

Three years after *The Emancipated*, which concentrates upon the spiritual side of the problem, Gissing studies the subject from a social angle, showing the difficulties middle-class girls meet with when they have to earn their living unaided, as well as the causes of woman's subjugation and the means to have her improve her situation. Two "odd women" set up a secretarial school to which only candidates of middle-class origin are admitted. Material independence is to be obtained through work, and women will have no support but their own. But many dangers are to be avoided on the way to equality with man: prominent among them are sentimentality, false education through worthless reading, and want of professional qualification. In order to succeed woman will have to stand her ground and fight man's attempt to keep her under his sway. Monica Madden will rue her disregard of such elementary principles: in order to free herself from shopwork, she thoughtlessly marries a man twice her age who turns out to be a jealous tyrant in matrimony.

Suffragettes were still to come, but Mary Barfoot and Rhoda Nunn would not have been disapproved of by them. When women have grown to be rational, responsible beings, they will gain access to all occupations. Gissing voices his irony through the progress of the plot: in the first chapter of *The Odd Women*, Dr. Madden dies in an accident, just after informing his six daughters of his intention of buying a life insurance. He thought that girls, in their education, should be spared the preoccupations of everyday life and nurtured on literature, and now his daughters are brutally confronted with the very problems their father had wilfully kept away from them. Another ironical touch is when Rhoda Nunn fails to accept free union with Everard Barfoot—a solution she herself had advocated. Even among the leaders of the movement, daring is limited and resolves cramped by tradition.

Few of Gissing's women take an active interest in politics, but in the borderland between the social and the political we find some of them engaged in philanthropy, a rich lady's or a clergyman's interest. In *Workers in the Dawn* the daughter of an Anglican clergyman who has become an agnostic devotes her money and the little strength left her by consumption to slumming. A free-thinker, she meets with distrust and treachery on the part of the poor, with selfishness and intransigence on the part of the Church of England. In *The Unclassed* Ida Starr, after she has inherited from her grandfather who died of cholera caught in the slums, spends her money to relieve the misery of the children of the poor. So does Mrs. Ormonde in her Eastbourne estate, in Gissing's most sentimental novel, *Thyrza*. He gives his philanthropists the idealism and generosity inspired by the wretchedness of the lower classes, whose coarseness and vulgarity shattered his own commiseration. Whilst commending the disinterestedness and patience of these women, Gissing makes quite clear the inefficacy of the system and it is significant that in his last and best novel of the lower classes, *The Nether World*, the philanthropic scheme eventually falls through. In his letters he forcibly attacks the neglect of government in social matters; clearly, in his opinion, the charity of humanitarians, however generous it be, is but a remedy ludicrously out of proportion with the evil it is meant to cure. Gissing, a true Victorian, is a moralist who takes delight in observing human conduct. He is at his best when he describes the moral degradation of a woman under some outward influence: money, drink, narcotics or the baneful attraction of London high life; or the mental unrest created by some new deep-reaching theory as in *Born in Exile* where Darwin's and Spencer's ideas are brought to bear on the gentle, traditionalist spirits of Sidwell Warricombe and her mother. Hide-bound philistinism he associates with provincial life. *The Emancipated* deals with the religious side, whereas *Denzil Quarrier* (1892) and *The Paying Guest* (1895) focus almost

103

exclusively on social formalism. It must have required him some effort to make a satirical or humorous presentment of these manifestations, as we know that in ordinary life he was easily infuriated by ignorance or beliefs he did not share. Thus in a letter to Ellen: "If only you would read *Phases of Faith*—a most minute history of spiritual slow emancipation, written by Cardinal Newman's brother long years ago. It would enable you to understand the all but frenzy with which I regard forms whose persistence is due to literal and absolute ignorance, and nothing else."[13] Charlatanism and narrow-mindedness of all kinds he pillories from *Workers in the Dawn* to *Ryecroft*.

If Gissing has any hope of seeing a beneficial evolution, it lies in education; but there again he has a clearer view of the pitfalls on the uphill road to improvement than of the panaceas in which, as a writer of fiction, he professes no interest. In *Demos* he declares war on authors of bad novels, whose mawkishness favours a naively romantic view of existence as well as women's natural waywardness and inconsistency. Let them be strangled and thrown into the sea! They deliberately choose to confuse love and sexual instinct and of the latter they dare not speak. Nor does formal education find grace in his eyes: *In the Year of Jubilee*, Jessica Morgan has crammed such uselessly arid learning into her poor, parched brain that she collapses during matriculation. In her delirium she repeats Samuel Barmby's suavely balanced phrase with unconscious irony: "The delicacy of a young lady's nervous system unfits her for such a strain."[14] Like his hero Godwin Peak, in *Born in Exile*, Gissing has no sympathy for blue stockings or radical-minded women. There appears his conservatism, along with one of his many paradoxes: he wishes for woman's emancipation, but as he realizes that it will be achieved at the expense of her femininity, Gissing stands abashed at the consequences of his own suggestions. The education he would like her to receive would be liberal and harmonious; it would consist in a sort of exclusively literary humanism, for the development of science anticipates evils of all kinds.

5

In addition to the marked influences his private life had on Gissing's view of women and on the shifting tone of his work, while he makes his point artistically and covertly by repeated representation of scenes and characters rather than by overt, didactic statement, other influences also conditioned his portraits of women, the tone with which they are presented, and the degree of aggressiveness with which he represents his attitudes. In the description of physical passion, for example, he never dared to violate the canons of Victorian morals: the publishers, critics and circulating libraries, Mudie's in particular, had frowned upon the audacity of social theses in *Workers in the Dawn* and *The Unclassed*. That Gissing had chosen prostitutes as heroines was an unusual piece of boldness for which he paid dearly in the few reviews of his books or the prudish silence of editors. He was painfully struggling against taboos. In 1884, he wrote a letter to the *Pall Mall Gazette*, which had just published an article by George Moore entitled "The New Censorship of Literature" directed against the libraries. Gissing accused novelists of sacrificing their artistic conscience to their love of money: "English novels are miserable stuff for a very miserable reason, simply because English novelists fear to do their best lest they should damage their popularity, and consequently their income. One of the most painful confessions in literature is that contained in the preface to *Pendennis*, where Thackeray admits that 'since the author of *Tom Jones* was buried no writer of fiction among us had been permitted to depict to his utmost power a man', on penalty, be it understood, of a temporary diminution of receipts."[15] This very sound protest was the object of a satirical article in *Punch* which besides throwing ridicule on Gissing's name ("A kind of guttural German embrace performed by the nationaliser of the Land") charged him with a taste for dirty literature.[16] That Gissing found these bonds galling is confirmed by Morley Roberts, to whom he complained that any illicit liaison had at least to be covered up by bigamy. Yet, despite his complaints, one must notice that he did not fully avail himself of the increasing broadmindedness of the 1890s. In that respect, a comparative reading of *The Whirlpool* and Somerset Maugham's *Liza of Lambeth*, both dated 1897, helps us to realize how moderate Gissing was in the description of love scenes.

Another qualification to his naturalistic bent lies in his occasional lapses into melodrama of Dickensian origin. At times the natural development may be slightly warped by one Mrs. Ormonde (*Thyrza*), one Mrs. Borisoff (*The Crown of Life*) or, worse still, one Mrs. Damerel (*In the Year of Jubilee*) whose interventions as *dea ex machina* deflect the action from its natural course. Invariably they smooth down—or obstruct—the way of some wished-for or obnoxious marriage. Such creatures thrive in French or English popular fiction of the nineteenth century but rank rather low on the scale of psychological plausibility.

In addition to their literary merit, his portraits of women have a value of their own as documents of social history. One finds in his novels a series of educated girls who have partly freed themselves of family and personal shackles and are courageously striving to attain equality of opportunity with the male sex. Of course, the seamy side of that attitude is a certain arrogance, a rather vulgar taste for adventure, a marked striving for material ends, but such women as Rhoda Nunn or May Tomalin stand as pioneers in the struggle for emancipation. Gissing's place as a portrayer of that movement is now safe: *The Odd Women* enjoyed a less boisterous success than Grant Allen's *The Woman Who Did*, but one of more sterling quality. A doubt sticks in his mind; when material and moral emancipation have been achieved there remains weakness to temptations of all kinds; with Alma Rolfe and Sibyl Carnaby in *The Whirlpool*, the way to freedom does not lead to the palace of wisdom and Gissing would not have refused to accept Sir Austin's statement in *The Ordeal of Richard Feverel*: "I expect that woman will be the last thing civilized by man."[17]

His ideas on woman, like his reflections on democracy and science bring him to a dilemma: disgruntled at the mediocrity of the present, he is yet distrustful of progress. The evolution of woman is necessary, but it threatens those female virtues in which he has great faith; similarly the evolution of the working class at large seems inevitable, but government by the people, whose coarseness he resents, would prove disastrous; again, the intellect is fascinated by science but science means war and he foresees a series of catastrophes originated by the human brain. These dilemmas or dichotomies are also borne out by the fact that at times a harshly realistic tone threatens to break through the dominant idealism whereas at other times an idealistic tone struggles to emerge through the dominantly realistic one.

Similarly, an audaciously critical attitude toward society seems constantly at war with a conservative point of view partly inherent and partly forced on him by pressures from without. The result, broadly defined, is that the lives of his characters, especially of his women, assume the form of a monotonous, relentless, undramatic tragedy.

NOTES

1. *Diary*, 25 August 1889. Quoted by Arthur C. Young (ed.), *The Letters of George Gissing to Eduard Bertz* (New Brunswick, N.J., 1961), p. 71.
2. *George Gissing's Commonplace Book*, ed. by Jacob Korg (New York, 1962), p. 48.
3. *The Unclassed* (London, 1895), p. v.
4. In the short stories he published in the Chicago papers the two extremes between which he will waver are already apparent, though, as may be expected, the idealistic vein occurs more frequently than the realistic one, as for instance, in "An English Coast Picture" or "Gretchen".
5. *Demos* (London, 1886), vol. III, ch. III, p. 54.
6. In his shorter novels, *Eve's Ransom, Sleeping Fires* (1895), *The Paying Guest* (1895), and *The Town Traveller* (1898), Gissing either discards the subject altogether or treats it in an uncommitted, gently humorous way.
7. *Charles Dickens: A Critical Study* (London, 1898), pp. 133-34.
8. J.D. Thomas, "The Public Purposes of George Gissing", *Nineteenth-Century Fiction*, VIII (September 1953), 118-23.
9. *Murray's Magazine*, III (April 1888), 506-18.
10. It has been noted that Gissing cared little for children until he began to feel disquiet for his elder son Walter. Peachey's solicitude for his infant son, as well as Harvey Rolfe's, echo Gissing's own troubles.
11. *Born in Exile* (London & Edinburgh, 1893), Part the Second, ch. II, p. 138.
12. *Charles Dickens*, p. 143.
13. *More Books: The Bulletin of the Boston Public Library*, XXII (December 1947), 376-77, letter dated 7K. 3 April 1890.
14. *In the Year of Jubilee* (London, 1894), vol. II, Part Four, ch. II, p. 161.
15. *Pall Mall Gazette*, as rptd. in *Pall Mall Budget*, 19 December 1884, pp. 12-13.
16. "Gissing the Rod", *Punch*, LXXXVIII (3 January 1885), I.
17. George Meredith, *The Ordeal of Richard Feverel* (London & New York, 1935), p. I.

8

Gissing's Studies in "Vulgarism": Aspects of His Anti-Feminism

by LLOYD FERNANDO*

In the present revival of interest in and sympathy for the Victorians there has been no discussion of the undeniably hostile cast of Gissing's novelistic practice in the portrayal of women and women's issues. Because his novels, especially those of the nineties, draw very fully upon the contemporary scene, it has even been assumed that he was unambiguously sympathetic to feminist claims. "On this subject at least," his most recent biographer, Jacob Korg, declares, "Gissing's opinions were clear, consistent, and uncompromising. An enemy of the Victorian myth of the inferiority of women, he believed firmly that women were the intellectual and spiritual equals of men."[1] This essay argues that the opposite view is more tenable; it also examines the ways in which the novelist's art was adversely affected as a consequence. Certainly Gissing wished to see women given a wider general education, and he was concerned about their opportunities for employment. The fate of the large number of women doomed to a single life, as the population ratio of women to men clearly showed, engaged his sympathies. He is also on record as suggesting, more daringly, that "the only way" of effecting lasting improvements in the

* "Gissing's Studies in Vulgarism: Aspects of His Anti-Feminism" by Lloyd Fernando: reprinted from the *Southern Review*, pp. 43-52, by permission of the editors.

status of women was "to go through a period of what many people will call sexual anarchy".[2] The letters, regrettably, do not elaborate this last point but his novels—*Denzil Quarrier* (1892), and *In the Year of Jubilee* (1895), notably—make it quite plain that he entertained the proposal only to dismiss it with a degree of shallow flippancy. Gissing is the only important novelist of the period whose approach to emancipation looks rather more like reasoned animosity to the movement. This claim gains considerable weight when examined in relation to his dismay at the growing vulgarity of the society around him. That was the novelist's wider concern, and it is fairest to see the issue in its light.

1

It is never easy to separate the person from the author in Gissing's novels. The works embody a broad scepticism towards society in general which George Orwell labelled as "close to being reactionary".[3] Gissing resented long and deeply his exclusion from the privileges of superior social status to which he felt he had a natural right by virtue of his education and intellectual qualities. Individual frustration taken together with his disgust at the dilution of social and moral values on the wider scene found a creative outlet in the impecunious intellectual hero who figures in almost every novel. These young men are the "unclassed", pacing restlessly on the outskirts of a society they haved ceased to comprehend. They regard the women problem from a superior vantage point as emblematic of social decay. Perhaps by association, Gissing's heroines, seeking to free themselves from traditional restraints, reflect some of this wider restlessness as well. Gissing wrote, after all, about a class of miscellaneous people bewildered by their social and cultural displacement in a rapidly expanding society. That is the underlying general aim in all his novels which gives us pause. But his error was to depend on "vulgarism", as he called it, as the principal lens for focusing his concerns in the nineties. As we shall see, it proved to be an inferior prism, lending itself to the idiosyncrasies of his vision rather than correcting it. In the latter phase of his long career as a novelist it effectively aborted any promise of full greatness in his art.

While he genuinely wanted the lot of the poor to be improved, years of enforced intimacy with them had only aggravated his personal repugnance for them. "Without wishing to be harsh to these people," he declared, "you must recognise how utterly impossible close relations with them become . . . I fear they put me down for a prig, an upstart, an abominable aristocrat, but *que voulez vous?*"[4]

The provision of fresh and more widely spread opportunities for education and employment meant little, if any, difference to the concept of a graded community. "All classes will be elevated, but between higher and lower the distinction will remain."[5] This exceptional caution about fundamentals of social improvements stemmed from a fear of dilution in the quality of life and society, an apprehension which Gissing found increasingly confirmed. Education brought only "extending and deepening Vulgarity", he told Bertz. Convinced that "the gulf between the really refined and the masses" had widened and would widen still more, he fell back on his rather wishful concept of an intellectual aristocracy. He called it "an Aristocracy of mind and manners" which would not demean itself by contact with a society of deteriorating values.[6]

He regarded issues relating to the advancement of women in a similar light. He acknowledged feelingly—in a way that reminds us that he spoke from bitter personal experience—the effects upon woman of her depressed status. Comparing the average woman to "the average male idiot" he believed her condition could be redressed, in part at least, by education, not primarily to enable her to compete with men on equal terms, but for the greater well-being of society.[7] Again, the distinctions between higher and lower would remain. Throughout his life he did not deviate much from the opinion he formed in 1880 that:

> A girl's education should be of a very general and liberal character, adapted rather to expand the intelligence as a whole than to impart very thorough knowledge of any subject. General reading is what I should advise a girl to undertake; and that reading should certainly *not* lie in the direction of the Higher Mathematics or Political Economy.[8]

The letters to his sisters are full of fatherly advice, consistent

110

with these principles, about the reading and other pursuits they should be undertaking to improve their minds. He believed that the proper adoption of his counsels—he often detailed approaches to particular authors somewhat like a school-master—would in truth emancipate their minds. In his letters to them he is a strangely silent, however, on other topics relating to feminine emancipation, notably women's relations with men. Arthur C. Young rightly points out that Gissing's prescriptions in fact aimed at producing the kind of refined woman he always had as an ideal, too far above him socially to be approached with love.[9] Neither sister married.

References to reading, art and learning serve as significant pointers to the moral quality of the women characters in his fiction. The Peachey household (*In the Year of Jubilee*) is especially detestable for its evidence of half-education in the form of "cheap miscellanies, penny novelettes and the like" which lie scattered about. Gissing never once conceded, expressly or tacitly, that women are the full moral and intellectual equals of men. His heroes, with their author's approval, patronise their women, assuming a natural superiority in all important matters. Waymark, Quarrier, Barfoot, Tarrant, Hilliard, and Rolfe (in *The Unclassed, Denzil Quarrier, The Odd Women, In the Year of Jubilee, Eve's Ransom,* and *The Whirlpool,* respectively) all smugly accept the premise that, on the whole, women fall short of men in intellectual and, therefore, moral quality. Intellectual power and breadth of knowledge were the sole indicators of superior moral worth. these were male virtues rather than female. Only at the end of a life finally mellowed by his association with Gabrielle Fleury, did Gissing recognise the fallacy of equating intellectual capacity exclusively with moral fibre. "Foolishly arrogant as I was," he declared,

> I used to judge the worth of a person by his intellectual power and attainment. I could see no good where there was no logic, no charm where there was no learning. Now I think that one has to distinguish between two forms of intelligence, that of the brain, and that of the heart; and I have come to regard the second as by far the more important. I guard myself against saying that intelligence does not matter . . . But assuredly the best people I have known were saved from folly not by the intellect but by the heart.[10]

111

But by then—1903—his score or more of novels had already been written.

2

The real mark of Gissing's resistance to emancipation rests in the way he linked the discordant social reality around him with the feminist movement, and in the way he implied in his novels that emancipationist ideas gave direct rise to the social vulgarity he detested. His novels of the nineties—*Denzil Quarrier* (1892), *The Odd Women* (1893), and *In the Year of Jubilee* (1894), for example—reveal his gradually increasing skill, and the limits to which he succeeded, in embodying his views in valid artistic ways. *The Odd Women* and *In the Year of Jubilee*, projected simultaneously, resemble each other closely. Each was to be "a study in vulgarism—that all but triumphant force of our time." He wanted, as he acknowledged in a letter to Bertz, "to deal with the great question of throwing pearls (i.e. education) before swine'," adding, pointedly, ". . . women will be the chief characters."[11] His presentation of the Madden sisters in *The Odd Women* is not completely the unambiguous expression of his sympathy for single women which it may be taken to be; they were also to symbolise the growing vulgarity of society. In the event Gissing failed to achieve this second aim, but the attempt to associate vulgarity with the supposed intrinsic feebleness of female nature has undeniably left the spinsters, especially Alice and Virginia, more pitiably repellent than they need have been.

As for the career-feminists whom he knew, he could resist distinguishing them from something called, at the time, "the womanly woman". In his novels they affect a mannishness of bearing, their countenances betray incipient masculinity. They are either guilty by innuendo like Mrs. Wade who is partly blamed for Lilian's death in *Denzil Quarrier*; or under the tutelage of a typical Gissing hero they rather unconvincingly acknowledge the folly of their ways, like Rhoda Nunn in *The Odd Women*, and Nancy Lord in *In the Year of Jubilee*. Particularly in the case of Rhoda Nunn's contest with Barfoot over their proposed marriage-experiment, an excellent opportunity was lost of illuminating love as a compulsive duel of the sexes, as Strindberg had done in his play, *The Father*, only six years previously. But Gissing was too close to the stuff of life he dealt with. Confronted by domestic and moral turmoil, he recoiled with loathing from the tawdriness of the "emancipated" women whom he saw as the cause of it. "Wherever you look nowadays there's a sham and rottenness; but the most worthless creature living is one of these trashy, flashy girls," old Mr. Lord says,

> the kind of girl you see everywhere, high and low,—calling themselves "ladies",—thinking themselves too good for any honest, womanly work. Town and country it's all the same.
> They're educated; oh yes, they're educated. What sort of wives do they make, with their education? What sort of mothers are they? Before long there'll be no such thing as a home. They don't know what the word means. (*In the Year of Jubilee*, Pt. I, Ch. V)

These novels are curious hybrids reproducing, virtually unchanged, contemporary views on feminist issues, but sustained on a literary level by Gissing's skill, discussed below, in older techniques of narrative and characterisation. The marriage histories portrayed have a kind of seedy authenticity. Few could know better than Gissing the bitterness that could arise among maladjusted couples. One of his earliest successes with this theme was in *The Unclassed* (1884) where he produced a chilling though abbreviated picture of a sensitive man's mortification in a bond which nullified every normal human feeling. Here Gissing was also at the heart of perhaps the most intractable moral problem of the age: the seeming unsuitability of the traditional conception of marriage in an era where ideals and duties were changing rapidly. He presented the impasse in marriage again in *The Odd Women* in the story of Widdowson and his wife Monica, the third of the Madden sisters; while in *In the Year of Jubilee* he showed how wide the gulf between husband and wife could be in his portrayal of the half-demented Ada Peachey and her husband Arthur. These marriages, forming important sub-plots, serve as the unamenable reality against which emancipationist theories were tested. No progressive theory could have much value which failed to alleviate this seemingly repetitive and harassing phenomenon. In his novels, Gissing brought these failed marriages into progressively closer contact with his feminist themes. His manner of doing it, however, reveals the limitations

113

of his grasp of the issue of marital incompatibility. Largely influenced no doubt by his own harrowing experiences, he roundly blames the woman in each case for prejudicing the stability of the relationship. The men would be able to do the world's work, or pursue the ideal of secluded and cultured living, he seems to say, if only the women did not seek an exaggerated degree of independence in their lives. His partiality for the male point of view was offset, however, by the authenticity of his depressing histories, a quality which appreciably increased the literary merit of the novels. When in *The Whirlpool* (1897) Gissing at least dealt centrally and at three-volume length with a foundering marriage-relationship, he had therefore devoted much thought to the problem and had the benefit of repeated preparation, as it were, for its literary presentation. *The Whirlpool* is Gissing's most skilful novel in every respect, but it has rarely been discussed. It embodies his mature vision with a technical assurance that must rank it very high among novels of the final decade of the nineteenth century.

In his delineation of the marriage of Alma Frothingham and Harvey Rolfe in *The Whirlpool*, Gissing at last mingled successfully his views on feminist ideals with those on marriage. "The theme is the decay of domestic life among certain classes of people and much stress is laid upon the question of children," he wrote.[12] Originally he planned to title his novel "Benedict's Household", which further confirms that he had given up interest in theoretical marriage-experiments for their own sake. He told H.G. Wells that in the characterisation of Rolfe, "I wished to present a man whose character developed with unusual slowness, and who would probably never have developed at all, after a certain stage, but for the change wrought in his views and sentiments by the fact of his becoming a father.[13] The novelist had clearly subdued any trace of a desire to be merely polemical in his approach to the issues of the day, and now wished to make a mature examination of a basic responsibility. At first, Harvey Rolfe adopts the position of an opinionated male intellectual with assured means. "People talk such sentimental rubbish about children," he says, ". . . they're a burden, a hindrance, a perpetual source of worry and misery. Most wives are sacrificed to the next generation—an outrageous absurdity" (*The Whirlpool*, Bk. 1, Ch. II). He is drawn gradually into the whirlpool of society; rather as Lydgate succumbed to Rosamund in George Eliot's *Middlemarch*, Rolfe slides into marriage with Alma Frothingham (Bk. 1, Ch. XI). His child awakens him to a sense of parental responsibility and to the general problem of educating children for a society which had lost much of its sense of tradition. It also brings him to a realisation of limits that must be drawn to a woman's independence, since Alma, nervously wrapped in the pursuit of her musical career and in the social life accompanying it, leaves her domestic relationships to founder as they may, or uses them to further her own ambition. As in *In the Year of Jubilee* and many of his previous novels Gissing sought again to enforce a didactic conclusion: that a woman could not be fully emancipated without baffling her husband in his efforts to make their marriage successful. In *The Whirlpool* the author's point of view, while still remaining obvious, is woven with far greater skill into the novel's substance. Here, a reader may disagree with the view but would nevertheless concede that the novel's considerable worth is not thereby greatly affected. Gissing eschewed author-intrusions, and his strict dramatic presentation, interweaving narrative, feminist opinions, and character, proved to be highly effective. It is fairest to look for the summation of Gissing's views here more than in his other novels.

His principals are well matched. Their marriage begins, for once, on terms of full equality, the fundamental demand of the feminist. But Alma's plans to embark on a career as concert violinist gradually estrange her from her husband, and their relationship thins steadily over two or three years into a tense and brittle cordiality. On the professional level, too, Alma progressively loses command over her power to make independent decisions, and fails to realise the vulnerability of her imagined freedom. In social circles she finds her self-respect set at nought. Felix Dymes, a hack composer and impresario, invites her to be his mistress. Cyrus Redgrave, the millionaire, patiently mines her path with subtle favours with the same objective. Alma herself soon becomes adept at using her admirers for her own purposes until the socialite Mrs. Strangways, in reality Redgrave's go-between in his amours, places her in the compromising circumstances that lead to

Redgrave's death. Alma retains just enough control over herself after this event to give a moderately successful recital, and then suffers a nervous breakdown. Events thereafter reveal the innumerable venalities she has committed at the expense of others to satisfy her own ego. Gissing's own accents are not far away in Rolfe's realization of how little his interests had mattered to her:

> Herein, of course, Harvey did but share the common lot of men married; he recognised the fact, and was too wise to complain of it even in his own mind. Yet it puzzled him a little, now and then, that a woman so intelligent as Alma should in this respect be simply on a level with the brainless multitude of her sex. (Bk. 3, Ch. VI)

Through Rolfe, Gissing reasserted his belief in the permanence of marriage as a fundamental social institution and in the incontrovertible superiority of men over women. Remarkably unoriginal conclusions after decades of moral tumult.

For all his skilful presentation of character, that of Alma Rolfe shows a bias against the independent woman impossible to ignore. Alma is a completely negative character. Where Rolfe is a scholar, she is mediocrity not only in learning but in her art even; where he is generous and understanding, she is actuated by petty jealousies and unrelieved malice. Every setback that she suffers, each new act of compromise, serves for Gissing as a fresh item in an accumulating body of evidence illustrating her folly. To put it crudely, he gives her enough rope to hang herself, and she does. Gissing told an absorbing story but he sacrificed, unwittingly, any claim to expose Alma as representative of her sex.

It is worth recalling that contemporary criticism of Gissing's novels was far more stringent than ours to-day. He ruefully admitted that "the public commonly speak of me as a 'woman-hater'!"[14] Gabrielle Fleury, the one woman who brought him a measure of real happiness, evidently needed some reassuring on this score, and Gissing was compelled to a strenuous, revealing disclaimer: "Gabrielle, once and for all let me tell you that I recognise no restraint whatever upon a woman's intellect. Don't judge me in this respect from my wretched *books*—which deal, you know, with a contemptible social class for the most

116

part."[15] But it was the books he was judged by. *The Saturday Review*, in a critique of *The Whirlpool*, declared, "Our women folk are not all angels, but . . . they are not invariably fools, wantons, sneaks, and nagging sluts. Mr. Gissing's sustained snarl at the sex at large grows a shade wearisome, not to say vexatious."[16] However, the *Bookman's* moderately argued reaction came much closer to the point:

> While we acknowledge his fine care in the representation of (Alma), we feel that we are reading a conscientious schoolmaster's report. Over and over again a more sympathetic interpretation occurs to one. For he is a pedant to human nature. Some temperaments when he touches them ring always false or sound flat. No novelist has taken more pains to understand the condition of the average woman's life today, to study her ambitions, to mete out to her an austere kind of justice. But the schoolmaster in him is ever deploring their methods . . . And so the best of his women are not women at all, but illustrations out of a treatise on the times.[17]

The portrait of Alma Rolfe confirms also Gissing's ultimate bafflement by the sex, his realization that for all his experience and all his theories there existed a residual mystery about women which he would never fathom. *Eve's Ransom* (1895), the one-volume novel immediately preceding *The Whirlpool*, had anticipated this final position with both neatness and economy.

While *The Whirlpool's* artistic merit makes it an extremely readable novel, it is also something of a literary curiosity: a well-nigh perfect Victorian three-decker, reappearing nearly twenty years after its vogue had properly ended. It was in fact published as a single volume, but its format in three Books corresponds to the old three volumes. The stuff of the plot consists, as that of much older fiction did, of simple misunderstandings, e.g. Alma's unfounded suspicion that her husband has had a liaison with Mrs. Abbott, and culminates in a somewhat melodramatic murder, that of Cyrus Redgrave. The narrative, dispersed among a number of characters, proceeds at much the same deliberate pace which George Eliot had used to such advantage. Jacob Korg has already pointed out that Gissing imitated her in many respects.[18] The study of the foundering marriage of Alma Frothingham and Harvey Rolfe, the author's central concern, does not differ much in kind from that of, say, Rosamund and Lydgate. The discrimination of motive in the characters resembles George Eliot's in its reliance upon a relatively unsophisticated psychology but without her massive intelligence. Further, some of the moral problems that Gissing deals with are defined by compromising circumstances—e.g. Alma alone in the house of the bachelor Redgrave—rather than by conflicting individual inclinations. We have only to think of *The Unclassed* to recall that at the outset of his career Gissing had tried to understand the latter type of problem, and it would seem that he found it insoluble for he never went back to it in the novels which followed. Finally, as in older fiction, while the evocation of milieu is detailed, the complex social inter-relations themselves are again presented— in the symbol of the whirlpool—as inimical to human happiness.

Although Gissing's literary endeavours over seventeen years culminate rather ironically in a kind of throwback to an earlier type of novel in form, structure and theme, his people nevertheless belong clearly to their own period with its tumult of expanding trade, social climbing, loss of group cohesion, and uncertain standards of sexual conduct. The early chapters capture vividly the sense of the disintegration of English society into a meaningless whirl of barbaric influence. Gissing originally meant his novel to retain this scope throughout. Discussing its theme with Wells, he said, "I have come to recognise a course of things which formerly I could not—or would not—perceive; . . . I have a conviction that all I love and believe in is going to the devil; at the same time I try to watch with interest this process of destruction . . ."[19] However, as his characters developed he was drawn, unwittingly, once again to his favourite presuppositions and, as the *Saturday Review* pointed out in the critique already referred to, forgot all about his original central purpose in writing the novel. In Frank Swinnerton's view, the novel "resembles rather the stirring of muddy waters than the authentic whirlpool which the author aims at presenting."[20]

The portrayal of women aside, the novel deservedly won both critical and popular success. H.G. Wells drew attention to its remarkable contemporaneity. The change taking place in Rolfe's mind, he wrote, is sweeping over the minds of thousands of educated men:

It is a discovery of the insuffiency of the cultivated life and its necessary insincerities; it is a return to the essential, to honourable struggle as the epic factor in life, to children as the matter of morality and the sanction of the securities of civilization.[27]

Wells believed *The Whirlpool* revealed the quality of a beginning—perhaps a rather thoughtless remark to make of one who had been writing for nearly twenty years. Ironically, it turned out to be the opposite: it was the novelist's utmost—and final—effort of artistry.

Gissing is the only novelist of stature to embody in his fiction the attitudes of reasoned opponents to female emancipation at the time when the movement had finally made its impact on the day to day living of ordinary young women. He is much more than the social historian William Plomer makes him out to be[22]: his bitterness over the social changes he witnessed and the integrity of his attempts to understand them lend to even his limitations a harsh vividness which still communicates itself to us to-day. At the same time he is rather less than a major novelist because his focus is too close to his subject matter to permit a proportioned selection of detail or careful discrimination of essentials from ephemera. Strictly speaking his novels are problem-novels which, though far superior to the common run of examples in this sub-genre, still did not achieve full artistic stature in the way the problem-play did in the hands of Ibsen. It is not necessary to award Gissing bad marks for being anti-feminist *per se*. That, on balance, is what he was, and it would be patronising to think the fact needs to be glossed over especially since it was an integral part of his attitudes as a whole. There is no doubt that it gravely interfered with the novelist's selective process—even as uncritical partisanship of the opposite variety has now consigned numerous other novelists of the period to irretrievable anonymity. At least with Gissing, his perspective of wider social concern lifts him easily above the common rut. It is only when we examine the areas where this concern is attenuated by his residually *petit-bourgeois* presuppositions, including those relating to women, that we understand the peculiar place he occupies between major and minor novelists in the late nineteenth century.

NOTES

1. Jacob Korg, *George Gissing: A Critical Biography* (Seattle, 1963), p. 185.
2. *Gissing to Bertz*, p. 171, 2 June 1893. I have discussed the ethical challenge of the Woman's movement in late nineteenth-century England in a previous essay, "The Radical Ideology of the 'New Woman'", *Southern Review* (Adelaide), II, 3 (1967), 206-22.
3. George Orwell, "George Gissing", *London Magazine*, VII (June 1960), 41. A review, unpublished during Orwells's lifetime, on the occasion of the 1947 Watergate Classics reprinting of *In the Year of Jubilee* and *The Whirlpool*.
4. 21 December 1880 (Yale University Library), quoted in Korg, *Gissing*, p. 90. Similar views are expressed by the chief character in *Denzil Quarrier* (1892), ch. III.
5. *Gissing to Bertz*, p. 172, 2 June 1893.
6. *Gissing to Bertz*, pp. 151-52, 1 May 1892. See also *Gissing to Family*, pp. 168-69, 22 September 1885 and p. 371, 8 July 1900.
7. *Gissing to Bertz*, p. 171, 2 June 1893.
8. *Gissing to Family*, pp. 72-3, 30 May 1880 (author's italics). Again similar views are to be found in *Denzil Quarrier*, ch. VII.
9. *Gissing to Bertz*, p. XXX.
10. George Gissing, *The Private Papers of Henry Ryecroft* (1903), "Spring", ch. XVI.
11. *Gissing to Bertz*, p. 144, 16 February 1892.
12. *Gissing to Bertz*, p. 219, 9 May 1896.
13. *Gissing and Wells*, p. 47, 7 August 1897.
14. *Gissing to Fleury*, p. 42, 14 August 1898.
15. *Gissing to Fleury*, p. 36, 8 August 1898.
16. *Saturday Review*, L XXXIII (10 April 1897), 363.
17. *Bookman*, May 1897, 38-9.
18. Korg, *Gissing*, pp. 259-60.
19. *Gissing and Wells*, p. 48, 7 August 1897.
20. Frank Swinnerton, *George Gissing* (London, 1912), p. 112.
21. *Gissing and Wells*, p. 258, August 1897.
22. See his Introduction to the Watergate Classics edition of *In the Year of Jubilee* (London, 1947).

PART TWO
New Grub Street

1

Lower Depths of Literature

by ANGUS WILSON*

I have always found Gissing's *New Grub Street* the most unbearably poignant of all nineteenth-century novels. More unbearable, I think, than Zola's *L'Assommoir*, because Gissing's novels have only an occasional rather forced poetry and scarcely any humour at all.

The failed writers and scholars of *New Grub Street* who totter on the brink of starvation, who nurse their injured pride and lacerated sensibilities in barely furnished attics choked by London fog and nourished on carefully eked out slices of bread and dripping, do so amid the ugly surroundings of Gissing's clumsy prose and in the cold light of his intellect which denies them all those distorting shadows, fascinating, Gothic and poetic, that the wild imaginations of Dickens or Dostoevsky lend to poverty, and without which there seems to be no distance put between us, the readers, and human misery.

But the condition of Gissing's characters is worse than just miserable; there is no logical hope of relieving it. We know this, and it makes our pity the more painful. Gissing himself and his characters—fashioned, after all, in his own likeness—know too, and the force of their hopelessness gives an extra twist to the screw with which they torture themselves. From the 1870s, as Mr. John Gross points out in his excellent preface to this welcome new edition, serious writers, scholars and critics began

* "Lower Depths of Literature" by Angus Wilson: reprinted from *The Observer Review*, 21 May 1967, by permission of the editors.

123

to lose the large readership that Dickens and Thackeray and even George Eliot had known. Mass education was beginning to demand mass media. From then on, genius that would or could not compromise would need private means like James or Virginia Woolf, or patrons like Joyce; even to get a start it would need, like Shaw, to marry money.

In *New Grub Street*, Reardon, the classicist who is trying to stretch his imagination to the length of the three-decker novels demanded by Mudie's Library, and Yule, the "man of letters" whose articles on Lord Herbert of Cherbury or Harrington's *Oceania* are hardly wanted in the market of *Titbits*, are neither of them geniuses. They are men of talent without power, even if they wished, to extend that talent. Their demand for special consideration from a competitive community is absurd; their aristocratic distaste for the proletariat (especially the up and coming semi-literate) into whose squalid and brutish lives they fear to be sucked is arrogance: their scorn for the fashionable cultured world, into which their more adaptable, less scrupulous, less talented colleague Milvain is making his way, is a luxury they cant't really afford.

Gissing, who has something of that Darwinian distaste for sentimentalising poverty that was soon to bloom in the novels of Samuel Butler and E.M. Forster and in the plays of Shaw, spares himself and us none of the weak and feeble elements that prevent Reardon and Biffen and Yule from surviving; but, like them, his real distaste is for the uneducated mob. Yet for all that their demands on the community for special consideration are irrational, unjustified and reactionary. Gissing makes it impossible for us not to care for his characters, not to resent the insults and injustices, real or imagined, that they suffer in a vulgar world not to forgive their awful rancour and hatred towards the uneducated wives they have married for sexual needs in their youth and who are now scapegoats for their failure to rise.

Yule and his friends who prose away and backbite and jostle one another for the sale of an eight-guinea article are a jungle within a jungle; and yet they are also men who truly love the classics, who once could have written well if they had not had to write so much, men for whom in a manner, absurd but true, the British Museum Reading Room really is the sort of Republic of Letters that they imagine ancient Athens to have been.

For egalitarians and men of the Left nowadays, such disappointed, embittered, self-educated failures have an ominous aura of Fascism about them; and for men of the Right, no doubt, they are to be suspected as the breeding ground of Utopian discontent. Yet their dignity, their rectitude, their refusal to compromise and their love of letters are as real as the horrible circumstances to which they are condemned; they may not be men of genius, but they have sensitivity, taste and mental powers well above the people, rich or poor, whom they despise.

Mr. Yule and his British Museum cronies would probably not face the workhouse in old age today. Scholarship, at least, has many more nooks and crannies in universites to give shelter to the bookish, but the pressure of the mass market upon the creative is greatly more insidious and more urgent. A recent survey showed us that of creative writers in England two-thirds earn only a little over £300 a year by their writing. Like Reardon and Biffen, most of the men and women in the Grub Street of the 1960s are no more than talented. How can they expect any special concern for their dignities, sensitivities and minority "gifts"? The sympathy that Gissing compels from us is surely sentimental and impractical. Yet I strongly suspect that the disappearance into the abyss of these stiff-necked writers or their capitulation to mass needs will remove a general culture of the talented upon which both genius and the improvement of mass taste depend.

But Gissing's novel is far more than a tract for our times. It is the crown of his uneven fiction; a rare English novel in which the characters, however desperately, are concerned with ideas, a Strindbergian battle of the sexes, in which nevertheless the author, for all his own painful experiences with his wives, creates some of the most living and likeable young women in English fiction without a trace of patronage or sentimentality.

2

Book and Bookmen

by ANON*

"Letter from Smith & Elder", George Gissing noted in his diary on January 7, 1891. "They think *New Grub Street* 'clever and original' but fear it is too gloomy. Offer £150 I wrote at once accepting (eheu!)." The note suggests both the background of the novel and Gissing's reasons for writing it. He was intensely concerned with the literary world and the means of reaching honourable fame in it, and also indignant that his own careful writing ("At the end of a lifetime one will perhaps manage a page that is decently grammatical and fairly harmonious" he wrote to his brother at this time) should get so little reward. In fact the reward was far from negligible by the time he wrote *New Grub Street*. Mr. John Gross is slightly misleading when he says in a generally perceptive introduction that Gissing had been "averaging" £50 a book before *New Grub Street*, for his two previous books had earned £100 and £150. Multiply this amount several times to reach a modern equivalent and it will be realized that Gissing was, as he remained, a reasonably successful author.

Nevertheless, he did not regard himself in this light. Several demons sat on his shoulder. He might lose creative power and become unable to write, he might go blind, his health might worsen so that he turned into a permanent invalid. These fears appear in the fates of Edwin Reardon and Alfred Yule in *New Grub Street*, and to exorcize them he scarified the literary world of the time. As Mr. Gross says, it was a decade when "the communications industry first began to assume its modern

---

* "Book and Bookmen" reprinted from the *Times Literary Supplement*, 29 June 1967, by permission of the editors.

126

proportions", and one fascinating thing about Gissing's account of this world is the detail with which he describes it. How much will one be paid for an article in *The Wayside* or *The Current*? Will Fadge be able to retain editorship of *The Study* after printing a favourable review of a novel abused in the paper three weeks earlier? Is Hink's "Essay on the Historical Drama" likely to have any success? One might be playing who's in who's out at a literary cocktail party. It would be a mistake to think that Gissing viewed this world realistically. The editors of and contributors to literary magazines, in the 1880s or today, are not so time-serving nor so vicious as he makes them appear. They are more honest, and perhaps duller. But for Gissing those inside the charmed circle were by definition corrupt or worthless and those outside must have been defeated by their own integrity. The only exceptions are figures like Whelpdale who, after his novel has been "refused on all hands", becomes a contemptible servant of the new commercialism and ends as editor of *Chit Chat*, Gissing's counterpart of *Tit Bits*.

Into this half-imaginary world Gissing placed a half-imaginary self: Edwin Reardon, a novelist of integrity whose springs dry up so that he ceases to write. The portrait of Reardon the failure is contrasted to that of the successful literary journalist Jasper Milvain who maintains that "literature nowadays is a trade" and that the tradesman "thinks first and foremost of the markets; when one kind of goods begins to go off slackly, he is ready with something new and appetising". The book's power springs from the very lack of balance with which these main characters are seen. Reardon's behaviour is wretched judged by almost any standards. Unable to write and continually bemoaning his own condition and that of the literary world, he reproaches his wife Amy bitterly for her failure to love him. The idea that he has any responsibility towards Amy or should feel any affection for their son Willie ("the poor little fellow has no great place in my heart", Reardon says when he learns that Willie has diphtheria) never occurs to Gissing, and when eventually Reardon goes back to his job as a hospital clerk at twenty-five shillings a week, insists upon giving Amy half his money and appears before her shabbily dressed, he thinks with relish that she will now understand what it means to live on twelve and sixpence a week. Reardon's solution for his problems is a purely emotional one. Like Gissing he demands the healing power of love, and when practical Amy suggests that he should go away alone to the sea and try to write he regards this as one more proof that she does not love him.

The portrait of "Jasper of the facile pen" is similarly loaded. Jasper certainly behaves badly in his attempts to marry for money, but in other ways he is shown simply as a man who wants to put his writing skills to commercial use. Lacking original talent, he is still able to appreciate good work. He arranges for the posthumous reissue of Reardon's novels and writes an enthusiastic article about him—in Gissing's terms a final irony, but one likely to strike the reader as a small mark of virtue.

It is never possible to see *New Grub Street* without thinking of Gissing's own problems, but this increases rather than diminishes its power. Like Frederick Rolfe Baron Corvo he spun fiction out of his own life, but he did so far more effectively partly through his ability to set down the real world in which he lived in all its banal detail, but primarily because of the tender longing for a true human relationship expressed in all his best novels. It is not possible to acquit Gissing of the charge of priggishness often made against him (he defined *prig* in his Commonplace Book as "a word used by the vulgar to stigmatize a man who thinks"), but then it is not necessary. His defects, like priggishness and lack of humour, are more than balanced by the deep serious tenderness in his writing. He really had something to say about the condition of society and of humanity in the Victorian age, and in half a dozen books, among which *New Grub Street*, *The Odd Women* and *The Whirlpool* would certainly have to be included, he said these things with a passion that sprang partly from his own flaws of character and temperament. He is not one of the greatest English novelists, but in his own way and on his own ground he is unique.

3

Middlemen

by WILLIAM TREVOR*

If making a living out of writing is a tricky business, it's nothing like as tricky as it was: there aren't many contemporary men of letters who move from garret to cellar and are obliged to sell their clothes. When Gissing published his finest novel in 1891 an excursion into the literary jungle could easily prove fatal. Today the native hatchet-men are sharper than ever, but at least the adventurer knows something of what to expect: the area has been charted, a kind of order prevails.

Gissing wrote, not about professional novelists or indeed about any other kind of creative writer, but about those promoters or detractors who prefer to concern themselves with the work of others. His writers are academics at heart, even when they're plotting novels of their own. They are literary men in what is still, I think, the accepted sense of the expression: men in the middle somewhere, who feel that culture is their business and that by hook or by crook they're going to have a stake in it. In *New Grub Street* Edwin Reardon's novel-writing is a burden to him and he's only too grimly aware of its shortcomings. Today his involvement with literature would probably take another form altogether. In an age where the favoured hack-work is no longer the writing of Sunday school stories but the less arduous composition of advertising copy, there are also more suitable alternatives and better pickings for other kinds of writer. In his introduction to this edition of the novel John Gross reminds us that Reardon "has made a career

* "Middlemen" by William Trevor: reprinted from *The Listener*, 14 September, 1967, by permission of the editors.

129

out of preserving his integrity; what he does with it, what he actually writes, is of secondary importance." How much more happily he'd have preserved it in, for instance, the cloistered calm of academic life.

Another character, Biffen, dedicated to the production of a novel called *Mr. Bailey, Grocer*, is on a mission "of absolute realism in the sphere of the ignobly decent". "Why", wonders Mr. Gross, "when he would rather be arguing about Greek metrics, should he spend his days cataloguing the 'ignobly decent' doings of a grocer?" Because, I suppose, he saw himself as a professional of a kind: there was at least a chance that he might make a pound or two out of his practical attempt to prove the superiority of the form of literary expression he favoured. Nobody was offering much for arguments about Greek metrics; nor could Biffen see any other way of conducting his mission.

To me, *New Grub Street* is the great English novel about people mercilessly out of place. It is at once depressing and exciting, harsh, cynical, sad and immensely moving. Cheerfulness never breaks through, no one is happy for long. Gissing's bitterness, though more obviously evident in *The Private Papers of Henry Ryecroft*, is an essential commodity. It flavours the book and spoils only the character of Reardon, the figure most like Gissing himself. Through it one can feel Gissing's distaste for the literary scene and for many of the characters within it: for his own Alfred Yule, wrecked by hypocrisy and his hatred of the malicious editor Fadge, for Fadge himself, for Jasper Milvain, the literary wide-boy of the piece, for the bright, vulgar Whelpdale. "Literature nowadays is a trade", Milvain states, and "putting aside men of genius who may succeed by mere cosmic force, your successful man of letters is your skilful tradesman. He thinks first and foremost of the markets, when one kind of goods begins to go off slackly he is ready with something new and appetising." The inhabitants of the new Grub Street, adds Milvain, are "men of business, however seedy". He is speaking of himself: prototype of the organised middlemen who throng the literary world today.

4

Offensive Truth

by JOHN GOODE*

New Grub Street by George Gissing, introduction by John Gross

In a note on *Tess of the d'Urbevilles* in 1891, Hardy quoted St. Jerome: "If an offense come out of the truth, better it is that the offense come than that the truth be concealed." This comes at the end of a decade which saw the decisive estrangement of the "serious" novelist from "the reading public", and, as a direct challenge to the latter's prescriptive rights, it could stand as the slogan of protest for writers as diverse as Henry James and George Gissing as well as Hardy himself. The two books under review, together with James's *Partial Portraits*, are the major documents of the writers' struggle against the economic anarchy of the literary profession and the hardening efficiency of grundyism in the case of artistic "truth".

New Grub Street registers, with cumulative density and inclusiveness, the era in which, as John Gross says, the communications industry assumes integrity and popular demand. The consumer is hardly there, for the over-whelming impression is of writers, reviewers and publishers caught in an ingrown struggle for a market which is divorced both from human effort and from human need. The involved individuals become mere reflexes: thus the paranoiac critic moves compulsively from a scathing attack on a rival who has tried to revive Elkanah Settle to a lecture on the virtues of Shadwell. Even the strong man, Jasper Milvain, is successful because he is prepared to make himself a caricature of the trivial journalist.

* "Offensive Truth" by John Goode: reprinted from the *New Statesman*, 7 July 1967, by permission of the editors.

131

The social structure of the novel is fixed by the hero when he says, "Between wealth and poverty is just the difference between the whole man and the maimed", and his own predicament is a paralytic contradiction: "If I could write books as good as the early ones, I should earn money. For all that, it is hard that I should be kicked aside as worthless just because I don't know a trade." Gissing's objectivity is marked and it is disappointing that John Gross should lapse into the normal biographical mode of Gissing criticism and suggest that his "realism" is "a masochistic wallowing in the common-place". For the hero is a failure, not because of Gissing's neurotic self-doubts, but because his values crumble before the new, depersonalised reality. His concept of the whole man, like Arnold's best-self is nostalgic. One of the characters scornfully points out that the last thing the working-class reader wants is a novel about the working classes. But this ironically rebounds, for we have already seen the hero and his best friend in ecstasies over Greek accents. For them, as for the "quarter-educated mob", art is a withdrawal from the offensive truth.

The honesty with which Gissing renders this cultural paralysis makes *New Grub Street* enduringly impressive, but it also points to the reason why Gissing isn't a major innovator, in spite of the radical modernity of his insights. He can see through his hero but not beyond him, as the prose, with its strange, persistent lack of urgency shows:

> That she had really ceased to love him he could not, durst not believe; but his nature demanded frequent assurance of affection. Amy had abandoned too soon the caresses of their ardent time . . .

"Could not, durst not" is a merely rhetorical intensifier. More striking is the leisurely inversion of colloquial word order and the genteel latinity of "frequent assurance of affection" and "caresses of their ardent time". It's neither pompous nor euphemistic, but its elegance retreats from the grimness of what it is describing (the breakdown of a marriage), as the hero himself on his *New Grub Street* not only represents the cultural crisis of the eighties, it is also a product of it. Unable to transcend the values whose defeat he so honestly records, Gissing stays trapped in the vice of culture and anarchy.

5

A World of Literature: Gissing's *New Grub Street*

by JEROME BUCKLEY*

One of the many luckless authors who drift into George Gissing's *New Grub Street* is a wispy alcoholic named Sykes, who is writing his autobiography, "Through the Wilds of Literary London", for a provincial newspaper. Few readers, Sykes complains, will credit the grim veracity of his narrative: "Most people will take it for fiction. I wish I had the inventive power to write fiction anything like it." Gissing himself could have said the same for much of *New Grub Street*, where he depends far less on inventiveness than on his personal acquaintance with the London literary jungle.

On its appearance in 1891 the novel was both attacked and defended as a grimly "realistic" exploration of the lower depths of an urban society. Yet the "realism" is strictly limited by the author's well-defined interest in his narrow theme: the struggle for survival of the late Victorian man of letters. Gissing does indeed present sharp impressions of mean streets and dreary lodgings, but only as they contain the lives of his defeated protagonists. He shows no interest in the tribulations of the unaesthetic London poor, their resilience, courage, and laughter; he has no concern with social reform or political protest. He is repelled by indigence and its paralyzing hold on the illiterate unaspiring masses, and firmly convinced, like his

* "A World of Literature: *New Grub Street*" by Jerome Buckley: reprinted from *The Worlds of Victorian Fiction* (Harvard University Press, 1975) by permission of the editors.

Henry Ryecroft, that the average man born to penury cannot suffer so intensely as the impoverished artist, for the "intellectual needs" of most Englishmen are merely "those of a stable-boy or a scullery wench". His sympathy in *New Grub Street* lies with the sensitive, gentle Harold Biffen, a novelist celebrating the "ignobly decent", rather than with the drunken wretch whom Biffen abandons in order to rescue a manuscript from a burning hovel. H.G. Wells found Gissing himself lacking in "social nerve" and bumbling in all practical affairs, with "some sort of blindness towards his fellow-men, so that he never entirely grasped the spirit of everyday life." Gissing's "realism", if it is to be called such at all, does not reach far beyond his private and acutely self-conscious experience.

Within the limits of its vision, however, *New Grub Street* achieves a considerable range. Though not precisely a *roman à clef*, it offers us a veritable Dunciad of the early 1880s, and we may be sure that the aggressive Jasper Milvain, the gossipy Mr. Quarmby, the redoubtable, querulous Clement Fadge, and a score of others had their living counterparts in the new journalism. Whelpdale's *Chit-Chat* with its blatant appeal to the vulgarity of "the quarter-educated" clearly parodies *Tit-Bits*, the penny paper on which George (later *Sir* George) Newnes built his fortune. *The Study* and *The Wayside* evidently corresponded to familiar monthlies of the time, and *The West End* and *All Sorts*, representing popular weeklies, actually furnished the titles for new periodicals in the later nineties. Milvain talks knowingly of the demands of the new "market", and Whelpdale projects a quite modern literary agency with a variety of syndicated services. Alfred Yule, on the other hand, insists doggedly on the standards of an old-fashioned pedantic scholarship, and Marian Yule, his daughter and amanuensis, learns to regard herself as a literary machine and to deplore "the hateful profession that so poisons men's minds". From beginning to end we hear much of the jealousies of authors and scheming rivalries of publishers, of sharp editorial practices, commissioned articles, hostile reviews, rejected manuscripts, ephemeral successes, advertising puffs, libels, and always the drudgery of endless plodding hackwork. And over nearly all of the characters, at some stage of their careers, if not continuously, broods the huge dome of the British Museum, beneath which hosts of readers sit "at radiating lines of desks" like "hapless flies caught in a huge web, its nucleus the great circle of the Catalogue".

Though the detail with which this literary world is evoked is altogether vivid and convincing, the author's attitude toward it is a good deal less than completely objective. Gissing makes no pretense at maintaining the severe disinterest of the thorough-going "realist". Many of his opinions and reactions slip naturally enough into the copious shoptalk of his characters, their circumstantial accounts of their projects, aesthetic principles, and journalistic misadventures. But his presence is felt also behind the narrative and his personal judgement, either as direct commentary or as grim irony, not infrequently obtrudes upon the action. He is not above haranguing the reader with irritable sarcasm:

> The chances are that you have neither understanding nor sympathy for men such as Edwin Reardon and Harold Biffen. They merely provoke you. They seem to you inert, flabby, weakly envious, foolishly obstinate, impiously mutinous and many other things. You are made angrily contemptuous by their failure to get on: why don't they bestir themselves, push and bustle, welcome kicks so long as halfpence follow, make a place in the world's eye—in short, take a leaf from the book of Mr. Jasper Milvain? . . . .
>
> It was very weak of Harold Biffen to come so near perishing of hunger as he did in the days when he was completing his novel . . . He did not starve for the pleasure of the thing, I assure you. (Chap. 31)

Gissing seems to be indicting the reader as much as Amy Reardon when he describes her belated expression of sympathy for Biffen as "so often the regretful remark of one's friends, when one has been permitted to perish." We may guess the depth of his pessimism—outside the fiction—from his complaint, as cheerless as a remark by Hardy's little Father Time, that any pleasure he might have found in observing the antics of a baby was destroyed by "the thought of the anxiety it [was] costing in the present, and of the miseries that inevitably [lay] before it" And he may see a like morbidity in the novel itself in the author's identification of a literary hack and his threadbare wife ("They had had three children;; all were happily buried") or

135

even in the naming of an indigent surgeon ("I was christened Victor—possibly because I was doomed to defeat in life"). We are left in little doubt about Gissing's outlook, his loyalties, or the direction of his antipathies.

Written with such prepossessions, *New Grub Strret* hovers between embittered satire and a waveringly defensive sentiment. At first glance the satiric element may seem the more conspicuous. The novel was possibly conceived as Jasper Milvain's story, for it begins and ends with Jasper—his is the first voice we hear and his the last word. As the title of the opening chapter suggests, Jasper is "a man of his day": he is emphatically on the side of the "new", and his alignment determines his success, just as Reardon's commitment to the past underlies his abject failure. Jasper's presence, his characteristic gesture, provides a frame: near the beginning he reclines on a sofa, his hands behind his head, as his sister plays the piano; at the end he lies back "in dreamy ease", while his wife, Amy, widow of the defeated Reardon, plays and sings for him. He is preeminently the practical man, selfish, ambitous, adroit, shrewd in his estimate of competition, charming when amiability seems politic, caddish when betrayal appears profitable. He has no delusions of genius or even of great talent as a writer; his objectives are simple and cynical; "Never in my life," he tells Reardon at the outset, "shall I do anything of solid literary value; I shall always despise the people I write for. But my path will be that of success. I have always said it, and now I'm sure of it." Later he warns Marian Yule with the same bluntness, "I shall do many a base thing in life, just to get money and reputation . . . I can't afford to live as I should like to." Marian of course is unwilling to credit his admission, until her inheritance proves too meager to be useful to him and she finds herself accordingly sacrificed to his advancement. Though he is convinced that he can be pleasant if only he has money, his corruption actually increases with his affluence. The very day that the jilted Marian and her father, now blind and broken, leave London, Jasper publishes his calculated eulogy of Yule's old enemy Fadge, to whose post as editor of *The Current* he is shortly to succeed. In the end, when his time-serving strategies have been richly rewarded, he assures Amy, who is likewise practical, that he cannot regret his decision to abandon

136

Marian: "My dearest, you are a perfect woman, and poor Marian was only a clever school-girl. Do you know, I never could help imagining that she had ink-stains on her fingers . . . It was touching to me at the time, for I knew how fearfully hard she worked." We could scarcely ask a more caustic portrait of the cad as man of letters.

As the novel proceeds, however, the satiric intention yields to a stronger autobiographical impulse. Jasper, relegated before long to the background, where he pursues his vision of success, comes forward only at intervals as a foil to less opportunistic and more vulnerable characters. Some of these Gissing attempts to view with a measure of detachment and obliquity, for he diffuses and to some extent disguises his subjective concern. To Whelpdale, who is an essentially comic figure, he assigns his adventures in America, in retrospect more ludicrous than painful: his contributions to the Chicago *Tribune*, his brief career as photographer's assistant, and his resort to a diet of peanuts when penniless in Troy, New York. Alfred Yule, a sharply drawn study of a cantankerous pedant, reflects his respect for scholarship and his trying experience of marriage to a woman beneath him socially and intellectually—though good, long-suffering Mrs. Yule is a steadier, more devoted wife than the unfortunate Mrs. Gissing. With Harold Biffen he has a far less constrained sympathy. Often subsisting simply on bread and dripping, Biffen never escapes the dire poverty that Gissing himself knew at least for short periods. As Gissing once did, Biffen plods miles of London streets in the early morning to earn a pittance by tutoring so that he may spend the rest of the day working at his unprofitable novel. If the finished *Mr. Bailey, Grocer* is apparently not much like Gissing's fictions; it suffers similar censure from reviewers who see no excuse for his "grovelling realism" or his failure "to understand that a work of art must before everything else afford amusement". Biffen speaks for Gissing when he describes the dangers of refusing to compromise one's conviction in a world where sensibility can survive only by masking itself in "genial coarseness". And by his last desperate gesture, his death by his own hand, Biffen brings to quiet fulfilment Gissing's recurrent suicidal moods.

When Edwin Reardon, who is the real protagnoist of *New Grub Street* complains that he should have married "some simple, kind-hearted work-girl" instead of the genteel, ambitious, middle-class Amy, Biffen rebukes his fantasy:

> What a shameless idealist you are!. . . Let me sketch the true issue of such a marriage. To begin with, the girl would have married you in firm persuasion that you were a "gentleman" in temporary difficulties and that before long you would have plenty of money to dispose of. Disappointed in this hope, she would have grown sharp-tempered, querulous, selfish. All your endeavours to make her understand you would only have resulted in widening the impassable gulf. She would have misconstrued your every sentence, found food for suspicion in every harmless joke, tormented you with the vulgarest forms of jealousy.

Gissing here writes from sad experience, for Biffen, imagining what Reardon has escaped, pictures just such a union as Gissing endured—and indeed, at the time of writing, was about to repeat. But apart from his marriage to Amy, Reardon's career and character run remarkably close in most details to Gissing's. When we first meet him, Reardon has already reached thirty, the age at which Gissing began the novel. Like Gissing, he has had a sound classical education in a provincial town, has come to London to write, taken miserable lodgings in a back street of Tottenham Court Road, worked for a while as secretary in a hospital, and written several novels, one of which has been successful enough in terms of sales, to permit him a memorable trip to the Mediterranean. Like Gissing, he eagerly buys old books when he has a spare shilling and reluctantly sells them off when hard pressed for funds. And like Gissing, he is oversensitive to reviews, impatient with people, and badly affected by inclement weather. His conduct surely commands a measure of Gissing's respect. Yet his portrait is no mere exercise in self-justification: it rests upon a deep and far from complacent self-knowledge.

Biffen describes Reardon the novelist as "a psychological realist in the sphere of culture" rather than a devotee of graphic fact and vulgar circumstance; and Gissing himself, in presenting Reardon's character, is very much the psychologist, intensely interested in the analysis yet often clinically detached from it. Despite his manifest virtues, his insight, intelligence, and candour, Reardon is an insecure, unhappy man, subject to sudden revulsions of feeling, a creature of self-pity and irritable pride as well as meekness and compassion. His wrangling with Amy reveals him at his worst, both defiant and abject, now scorning the wife's practicality, now cringing before her common sense. He craves affection and is willing to grovel for it, but when his tears accomplish nothing, then "the feeling of unmanliness in his own position torture[s] him into a mood of perversity", and he becomes cruel in his angry retorts. Ultimately he nourishes his despair; in defeat he regards his seedy clothes "with pleasurable contempt" as "tokens of his degradation", and in the evenings once or twice a week the masochist of his emotions, he haunts the street where Amy is comfortably housed, so that he may go home hungry to his garret "with a fortified sense of the injustice to which he [is] submitted". His deterioration, paranoid or schizophrenic, is chronicled with an almost Balzacian power and dispassion: "An extraordinary arrogance now and then possessed him; he stood amid his poor surroundings with the sensations of an outraged exile, and laughed aloud in furious contempt of all who censured or pitied him." When we consider the extent of Gissing's identification with this lonely man, we cannot but be shaken by the terror of the self-appraisal.

Reardon's alienation, carrying him at times close to derangement, arises simply from his maladjustment to the new world of literature and his inability to admit the reality of any alternative existence. Gissing himself, though often disappointed at the reception of his books, was never so great a failure, and his extrapolated fears rather than his direct experience inspired his account of Reardon's collapse. Nonetheless, he shared his hero's commitment to the literary life and especially his literary enthusiasms. Like Reardon, he delighted in the Greek classics and responded warmly to the Greek setting as a reminder of the vanished ancient glory. From Athens in 1889 he wrote lyrical letters of the ruins glowing in the evening light:

The sunsets are of unspeakable splendour. When you stand with your back to the west and look towards the Acropolis, it glows a rich amber; temples, bulwarks and rock are all of precisely the

139

same hue, as if the whole were but one construction . . .
Impossible for you to imagine what I mean. Impossible for any
painter to render such scenes . . .
 One of the sunsets was rendered extraordinary by the fact
that, at the same time, there was a perfect rainbow circling over
the whole of Athens, from the foot of one mountain to that of
another: the colours of the hills were unimaginable.

A year later, writing *New Grub Street*, he granted Reardon the
same aesthetic satisfaction in almost identical terms.
Enraptured by the memory, Reardon tells Biffen of "that
marvellous sunset at Athens":

> I turned eastward, and there to my astonishment was a
> magnificent rainbow, a perfect semicircle, stretching from the
> foot of Parnes to that of Hymettus, framing Athens and its hills,
> which grew brighter and brighter—the brightness for which
> there is no name among colours . . . The Acropolis simply
> glowed and blazed. As the sun descended all these colours grew
> richer and warmer: for a moment the landscape was nearly
> crimson. (Chap. 27)

Biffen thinks it self-torture to remember such pleasures, but
Reardon insists that he is sustained by his lost dream: "Poverty
can't rob me of those memories. I have lived in an ideal world
that was not deceitful, a world which seems to me, when I recall
it, beyond the human sphere, bathed in diviner light."
Antiquity thus tempts him to escape the human sphere
altogether and so to transcend the concerns of a psychological
realism and all the demands of his own fiction, which by
comparison with the great classics seems "so wretchedly,
shallowly modern". And the past awoke a similar vain nostalgia
in Gissing himself; *By the Ionian Sea*, the most serene of his books
concludes with the sigh of the classicist manqué: "I wished it
were mine to wander endlessly amid the silence of the ancient
world, today and all its sounds forgotten."
 In both his commonplace book and the autobiographical
Henry Ryecroft, Gissing defines art as "a satisfying and abiding
expression of the zest of life". Yet, as Frank Swinnerton
observed, there is very little true zest in Gissing's own art and
little or no exuberance or striking vitality in his characters.
Reardon, convincing in his quiet despair, becomes intensely

animated only on the subject of Greece, but it is hard to imagine Reardon's novels, sensitive though they may be, as really zestful on any subject. Like Gissing, Reardon is apparently a careful craftsman with limited range. Gissing is indeed describing much of his own earlier work when he tells us that Reardon's stories, lacking "local colour" and exciting action, are "almost purely psychological" in interest, devoted as they are to the intellectual dilemmas of people of intellect. And even as he is chronicling Reardon's difficulties in padding out the second volume of a three-decker, he himself is facing the problem of inventing appropriate incidents to complete the three-volume structure in which Reardon has his being.

Though it self-consciously contains its own criticism, *New Grub Street* attempts a larger, more general literary statement. Like many later works of fiction and poetry, it concerns itself with the artist, the medium, and the aesthetic act; it is essentially a novel about novelists and the writing of novels. Throughout it is informed by a writer's understanding of the cruel demands of composition, the challenge of the blank page to be filled, the frequent recalcitrance of words, and the refusal of the torpid paragraph to come to life and move with grace and logic. When spared the grosser distresses of hunger and poverty, Reardon still knows the anxieties and frustrations of his craft: "Sometimes the three hours' labour of a morning resulted in half a dozen lines corrected into illegibility. His brain would not work; he could not recall the simplest synonyms; intolerable faults of composition drove him mad. He would write a sentence beginning thus: 'She took a book with a look of—'; or thus: 'A revision of this decision would have made him an object of derision'. Or, if the period were otherwise inoffensive, it ran in a rhythmic gallop which was a torment to the ear."

Gissing himself experienced similar woes, but also, we gather from his notebook, moments of a satisfaction usually denied to Reardon: "The pains of lit. composition. How easy any other task in comparison. Forcing of mind into a certain current, the temptation of indolence with a book. Yet the reward, when effort once made." His emphasis, however, falls less on the art of the novel than on the temperament of the novelist as a man apart, the sensibility that seeks creative expression and so

141

sentences itself forever to the discipline of an isolating and harassing creativity.

Harold Biffen, we are told "belonged to no class". Reardon, too, is an unclassed literary hero, aloof from the grades of society, fallen from a bourgeois economic status and dissociated in any case from philistine tastes and prejudices, living among the poor yet not of them, respecting the rare independent imaginative thinker, impatient with all vulgarity of thought or gesture. Both Biffen and Reardon could declare with Henry Ryecroft (and so with Gissing): "The truth is that I have never learnt to regard myself as a 'member of society'. For me, there have always been two entities—myself and the world—and the normal relation between these two has been hostile." Nonetheless, both draw the materials and settings of their art from the hostile society rather than from an imagination able to transcend or transmute the commonplace. Especially in studying Reardon, Gissing appraises his own attitude and practice with some dispassion and not wholly favorable judgment. *New Grub Street* at its best is a stocktaking rather than a naive apologia.

The Private Papers of Henry Ryecroft, on the other hand, which followed twelve years later, wears a thinner fictional disguise and suffers the burden of a more directly engaged self-defense. Spared Reardon's fate by a timely legacy, Ryecroft has retired to the seclusion of a Devon cottage, where he may cultivate his roses and cherish his solitude. "I do not enjoy anything nowadays," he insists, "which I cannot enjoy *alone*." Though he has rejected journalism as a "squalid profession" he has always valued the career of letters for "its freedom, its dignity". Self-absorbed and self-opinionated in his voluntary exile, he is now free to extol his difference from other men. He has escaped the London literary struggle for survival; but in withdrawing he has lost his subject matter. The most vivid of his papers record his sufferings as a young writer in the city, hungry days remembered with a proud self-pity and even a degree of nostalgia. In his aloneness he can now believe that all reality is subjective; that no one, for example, can share his memory of a Suffolk landscape, since, as he tells us "the place no longer exists, it never existed save for me. For it is the mind which creates the world about us, and, even though we stand side by side in the same meadow, my eyes will never see what is beheld by yours, my heart will never stir to the emotions with which yours is touched."

Though likewise personal and private in many of his reactions. Reardon has no such illusions about the real substance, the grim otherness, of the milieu in which Milvain and Fadge succeed and he and Biffen fail. If there is as much of Gissing in Reardon as in Ryecroft, Reardon nonetheless gains a solidity and dramatic independence as a character, far beyond Ryecroft's, from the cogent depiction of the intellectual setting in which and about which he must write. The physical conditions of authorship have surely changed in many ways since 1891, but the problems of the commercialization of literature and the challenge to aesthetic integrity, which Gissing recognized as never before remain real and inescapable. *New Grub Street*, the most obsessively literary of Victorian novels, leaves us no doubt about the objective reality of its world.

6

New Grub Street : An Approach Through Form

by JOHN PECK*

Gissing is a remarkably popular novelist with academics who want to write about something other than novels. Turn to any book on social history or cultural history in the Victorian period and Gissing is more than likely to be omitted. Of course this has more than a little to do with the nature of his novels; a point P.J. Keating makes clear in his useful book on *New Grub Street*:

> although some critics, most notably Q.D. Leavis and Irving Howe, have had no hesitation in proclaiming it a work of art, its continuing interest for the twentieth-century reader lies in Gissing's astute and probing analysis of the "business" of literature. First and foremost it is a sociological document; a sociological document of genius written in the form of a novel.[1]

This might be overstating the case, but it does describe accurately the nature of much of the critical interest in Gissing. However, recent developments in novel criticism, both in England and elsewhere, have shown a swing away from an approach through content and context, and an increasing emphasis on form. The question this prompts is whether Gissing will receive attention from those who wish to concentrate on the structural and linguistic qualities of fiction,

---

* *"New Grub Street*: An Approach Through Form" by John Peck: reprinted from *The Gissing Newsletter*, July 1978, by permission of the editors.

and who show nothing but impatience with the sociology of the novel. Quite simply, if formalism becomes central in the university teaching of fiction, will Gissing be pushed even further towards the fringes, remaining a subject of academic interest only to an ever dwindling minority?

Initially the prospects seem gloomy. In a formalist approach Gissing is of more immediate interest for his weaknesses rather than for his strengths. The shortcomings are easy to list. First of all he is a realist, which in the eyes of some proponents of structuralism is, of course, equivalent to saying that he is not worth bothering with at all. But the real problem with Gissing's realism is that it is often combined with a hectic plot structure. Even in *Born in Exile*, where the mechanics of the plot are less obvious than in many of his novels, there are things which arouse suspicion. In particular, Peak's imposture stands out as a piece of ingenuity, a plot device to make the novel happen, which we would not normally expect in a work in this mode. What one admires in a realistic novelist are the insights into character and situation on a vertical scale, whereas the horizontal progression of the story must be something we are all but unaware of, or subtle enough to match the local density. In Gissing the horizontal progression is frequently obvious and awkward. In reading *New Grub Street* for example, one's awareness of local insights and felicities is frequently marred by an awareness of the relentless progress of the plot. One's readiness to attest to the credibility of the material is undermined by an awareness of overwhelming artifice. Not that artifice is necessarily a bad thing. But it works, as in a Dickens novel or a Hardy novel, where it is deliberate, whereas Gissing all too often seems to be plundering the storehouse of recurrent situations simply in order to keep the thing going.

Another major problem in his novels, although this does not affect *New Grub Street*, is the old one of the narrator's voice in a work containing working class and must appear somewhat out of sympathy with the characters being presented. It is a problem which no novelist has ever really solved, but the unfortunate result for Gissing is that he might appear to be an awful snob, simply because of his preference for working-class subjects. It is the very lowness of his subject-matter which emphasises the superior manner of his own voice. *New Grub Street,* of course, does not present this problem, because the material is not at odds with the narrator's voice.

But there are problems with this novel besides the artificiality of its plot. One is the mechanical efficiency of Gissing's prose, evident as early as the first sentence: "As the Milvains sat down to breakfast the clock of Wattleborough parish church struck eight; it was two miles away . . ."[2] One can see what the sentence is achieving—the notion of a settled, ordered, community is immediately established through the reference to the church, and the choice of even, rather than odd, numbers. A sort of pastoral calm is conveyed in the name Wattleborough, and we already know a lot about the Milvains, because of the civilised regularity implicit in their taking breakfast at a set hour. But the objection to the sentence is that this complex impression is achieved by a cataloguing of facts which, continued over a long period, can become wearying. There is a lack of metaphoric richness to the prose, and when symbolism is used it seems obtrusive and clumsy. The first page, for example, contains the symbol of a hanged man, but it does not seem to jell with Gissing's preferred method of detailing information. The subsequent picture of Milvain waiting for the train to pass, with the all too apparent parallel of energy between the two, also seems forced, as if Gissing is only really at ease with the most prosaic style. And this prosaic style can seem dull and uninventive.

His language is not the final problem. The opening setting, and the first three chapters, are a piece of obvious pastoralism, which again seems to indicate a certain clumsiness in Gissing's handling of the work. It is not real countryside, but countryside derivative from literature, serving the function of idyllic retreat which countryside so often serves in art. And the dependence upon literary sources is even more obvious when we come on to the minor characters. Whelpdale, for example, is Dickens' perennial hopeless suitor lifted wholesale into another man's work. It is all promising material for the formalist, but material which can be used to denigrate Gissing. Not only do his plots lean upon earlier fictions, but his characters are also derivative.

Cataloguing a novel's shortcomings is a dreary, and not very admirable, critical activity, and it is now probably time to call a halt, but enough has been said to suggest that there are very real problems involved in assessing *New Grub Street* as a work of art. To summarise the problems, they seem to centre on a mechanically relentless plot, a flat prose style, a symbolic poverty, and derivative characterisation. The formalist might concede that the portrait of Reardon is remarkable, but this is only one element in a novel which, as a whole, can seem very shaky. This is the point at which it is tempting to suggest that the novel might have these faults, but that in emphasising them one is likely to overlook interesting things in the content of the work. The extension of this is to point to the limitation of formalist criticism which seems to blind itself to the intrinsic interest of novels for a sterile pursuit of abstractions; but the purpose of this article is to consider the novel from a formal angle, and it seems only appropriate to try and defend it in similar terms.

To make a start, there is one aspect of *New Grub Street* which offers a tempting promise to formalist critics, attracted as they are by novels in the Tristram Shandy tradition, that is, novels about novel-writing, and this is the possibility that the novel itself, in its form, is the perfect illustration of the problems about novel-writing raised in the content of the novel. That is to say, we understand Reardon through the experience of reading a work in which all the strains of writing a three-volume novel are in evidence. It is certainly tempting to emphasise the reflexive qualities of *New Grub Street*, and there seems no limit to the ingenious levels of self-reference a determined critic could discover in the work. But such a reading would seem ingenious rather than perceptive, for one very simple reason, *New Grub Street* is not a bad novel about writing bad novels because it is not a bad novel. However, the view that the formal strains in evidence in the work do add something to our appreciation of the content of the novel should not be dismissed completely. The only objection is to taking the argument too far, to transforming Gissing into a very different novelist from the one he obviously is. In order to defend the novel formally some more straightforward explanation of its formal strength needs to be sought.

In fact, the formal strength of the novel seems to be the frequency with which Gissing heads in a direction which is the mirror opposite of his formal weaknesses. It is most evident when one considers the relentless pace of the plot. Gissing, in his plot, seems reconciled to the simplest form of linear coherence, but at significant stages in the novel this tendency is brilliantly subverted. A novel which is full of action contains some of the best presented moments of inactivity in the whole of fiction. This can be seen in our first view of Reardon. After three brisk chapters of exposition, in which Reardon has been referred to on several occasions, we are suddenly confronted with the man himself:

> One evening he sat at his desk with a slip of manuscript paper before him. It was the hour of sunset. His outlook was upon the backs of certain large houses skirting Regent's Park, and lights had begun to show here and there in the windows: in one room a man was discoverable dressing for dinner, he had not thought it worth while to lower the blind; in another some people were playing billiards. The higher windows reflected a rich glow from the western sky.
>
> For two or three hours Reardon had been seated in much the same attitude. Occasionally he dipped his pen into the ink, and seemed about to write: but each time the effort was abortive. At the head of the paper was inscribed "Chapter III", but that was all. And now the sky was dusking over; darkness would soon fall.[3]

The obvious, and perhaps rather strained, contrast here is between light and dark: the contrast not really contributing much to the novel because of the lack of reticence so frequently in evidence in Gissing's more poetic writing. But it is a remarkable scene nonetheless, and is so because of its lack of movement, lack of progress, which contrasts so dramatically with the rapid pace maintained for the first three chapters. Up until this point words have rattled forth confidently, but here we are confronted with the novelist with nothing to say. The formal originality is that Gissing has dared to present the sterility of so much of the process of writing by bringing the novel to a complete halt, so that the only encounter is between a man and a blank piece of paper.

Frequently our insights into Reardon are achieved by this sort of formal device, but there is an added richness here due to the contrast with the world of activity. In the man dressing for

148

dinner and the people playing billiards we have a beautifully simple illustration of the world moving along in front of the artist, but the artist unable to enter this world of movement, either in his life or in his work. A scene like this shows up the inadequacy of Irving Howe's comment that *New Grub Street* remains in structure a Victorian novel, but the subject and informing vision are post-Victorian . . ."[4] Howe's comment is obviously suspect, because he seems to envisage the possibility of a quite amazing divorce of form and content, in which an old structure can contain a whole new set of perceptions. The obvious riposte is that if the informing vision is post-Victorian then the structure must be as well; and it is such things as these scenes of total inactivity which contribute to the formal and thematic originality of the novel.

Across the novel there is a readiness to experiment with structure in order to present the picture of Reardon, and these experiments always acquire increased force by contrasting so dramatically with the standard story-telling pace of the novel. There is, for example, the formlessness of Reardon's days, the description of which necessitates Gissing providing a fairly shapeless passage of prose, in contrast to the shaped structure of the work as a whole. His rows with his wife are similar in structure. They are circular rows, in which, if it were left to Reardon, nothing would be resolved. The point is that we come to know Reardon by contrasting this formlessness not only with the mechanical rigidity of Milvain's day but with the efficient inventiveness of the plot as a whole. Of course, the excessive linear coherence, the over-reliance on neat formulations of plot, can never be fully defended, but the other side of the coin needs to be considered as well. Excessive ingenuity of structure is frequently matched by a brilliantly innovative lack of obvious structure for passages featuring Reardon.

The consequence of these experiments with structure is a picture of Reardon of undeniable brilliance. But it is not only the structural originality that makes the portrait so impressive. There is also Gissing's irony, which affects the presentation at every turn. We are never allowed to lose sight of Reardon's egotism, his selfishness, his readiness to blame others for his failure. It is there in his attitude to his wife and child, and also in his relations with Biffen. An example is the scene of his first

149

encounter with Biffen after the fire which has destroyed the man's home, and nearly destroyed his manuscript. Biffen goes to Reardon's rooms at eleven o'clock at night and finds Reardon sitting by the fire. Biffen speaks first:

> "Another cold?"
> "It looks like it. I wish you would take the trouble to go and buy me some vermin-killer. That would suit my case."[5]

In spite of Biffen's near tragedy the conversation thus begins with a discussion of Reardon's problems, who seems too self-absorbed to wonder why his friend might have appeared so late in the evening. In addition, Reardon's conversation is marked by his usual maundering self-dramatisation. And this insistent self-reference is seen whenever he appears in the novel. Yet Gissing never labours the point. He never editorialises in his presentation of Reardon, but trusts to the action to reveal the man. Again we see the credit and debit quality of Gissing's form. His touch with his main character is as certain as it is uncertain with his presentation of minor characters, who are never presented with the same reticence. The conclusion on character presentation is the same as on the mixture of realism and obvious plotting in the novel. Although the novel is over frenetic in its plot there are moments, in the treatment of Reardon, where Gissing reveals a whole new sort of formal sophistication. Similarly with character, here is much in the novel which is derivative, but in the presentation of Reardon Gissing not only shows unusual restraint and artistry but manages to create a character who is radically new.

But where this ability to produce something running counter to his apparent imitations is possibly most in evidence is in the alleged prosaic flatness of his style, and the related lack of any effective symbolic dimension to the work. It is the flat style which creates the impression that it is "First and foremost a sociological document . . ." The implication is that a more flexible style could have led to a more complex novel. Of course, the portrait of Reardon does depend upon a more complicated style, a style which incorporates irony, and it would be absurd to describe the interest here as merely sociological. But it is possible to feel that the context in which he is presented is principally of documentary interest, because of the fact that the style in which it is presented is the fairly mundane descriptive style of the social historian. But it is possible to argue that there is a mode of aesthetic ordering in the novel which runs counter to the apparent descriptive method. That it has not been widely appreciated is, I think, due to the nature of the traditional content-based criticism the novel has received, which, finding what it wants to find, ignores other qualities in the text. Here is an area where a formalist approach can actually make Gissing seem a better novelist than even an admirer such as Keating would acknowledge.

The alternative mode of ordering in the book is symbolic, but not the rather forced symbolic moments, rather a more thoroughly integrated symbolic structure. It can be seen, for example, in the use of rooms in the novel. Milvain is presented as passing through a series of rooms. In fact, we hardly ever seem to see him in the same set of rooms twice, and we certainly never see him in his own lodgings. They are referred to, but never described, as this might suggest a sense of confinement inappropriate to his personality. Biffen we also see in a series of rooms, but he is oblivious of his surroundings. Whenever he arrives he immediately makes contact with the person without pausing to reflect on his surroundings. In the Yule household we get a sense of separate rooms, of a territory which is Mrs. Yule's, and of a territory which is Yule's, so that when Marian is summoned to her father's rooms there is a sense on his part of extending a privilege. But the character who is most sensitive to rooms is Reardon. We are alerted to this in his response to the British Museum reading-room, which he has come to love although at first it gave him a headache. If it had this effect it is only natural that more dismal rooms will oppress and upset him even more. And the novel makes full use of Reardon in drab and draughty rooms, stripped of furniture, and oppressively closing in on him:

> A street gas-lamp prevented the room from becoming absolutely dark. When he had closed the envelope he lay down on his bed again, and watched the flickering yellowness upon the ceiling.[6]

This makes an impact in itself, but the effect is reinforced by the chapter almost immediately concluding, to be followed by a chapter beginning, "The rooms which Milvain had taken for himself and his sisters were modest, but more expensive than their old quarters.''[7] Gissing does not need to underline the fact that as Reardon becomes progressively more confined Milvain finds space to expand. There is, though, a curious ambivalence in Reardon's attitude to the rooms he occupies. He sees them as representing his isolation and loneliness, but they also attract him because they offer the seclusion he craves. So rooms in the novel present a threat but also represent privacy.

The dome of the reading-room also seems to carry the same dual significance. It provides a sheltering roof for the devoted scholar, but it is also an umbrella to a whole network of human problems. It is perhaps only for Reardon that the reading-room represents nothing but a retreat, and a significant feature of the novel is that we never see him at work there. It is those for whom the dome does not have the power of sanctuary who are presented undergoing their daily toil beneath its shadow. It is under the dome that Marian sees Milvain, and it is under the dome that the infighting and politics of the literary world are conducted. It also acts as a central symbol, though, through the sense the novel gives of the reading-room being the hub of a web of literary activity. The novel conveys a clear impression of a grid imposed on London with literary activity in remote parts.

Indeed, a frightening sense of London emerges in the novel. From Reardon's rooms we might glimpse fine views in a pastoral distance, but London itself is hot and polluted, or else cold and foggy. But it is always a London where people wander aimlessly in the streets, or find themselves trapped in lonely rooms. Throughout the novel we gain a sense of people lost in a gigantic maze. Streets and rooms proliferate to the point where we are overwhelmed, and the sense of place is generally confusing and threatening. Frequently what dominates in the novel is not a sense of character, but a sense of alien and changing environments. And there is no escape from this bewildering jungle as the pastoral calm has been left behind in the first three chapters.

Throughout the novel, then, we are wandering through mean streets into bleak and unwelcoming houses. And this sense of a huge unmanageable city is also conveyed by the inclusion of many characters who are referred to but never seen. The object of this is not inclusiveness, but to increase the sense of an anonymous city. The idea of a traditional community, where everybody knows everybody, and where breakfast is at eight o'clock, and where the church is exactly two miles away, is accordingly destroyed. Consequently, Gissing's flat prose style has to be seen not as the norm, but strategic. It is a way of carefully and confidently delineating experience so that he can play off against it a far more intangible sense of the world his characters occupy. As a whole the novel does not present a documentary account in the appropriate style, but moves from this to a sense of human existence which can only be suggested by symbols such as the dome, and rooms, and streets, and London. The accusation of prosaic flatness thus crumbles, for the novel moves beyond realism towards symbolism. But it is a level of richness in the text which can be overlooked if one is too insistent on seeing the novel as a documentary account of literary London.

In fact, by emphasising this formal dimension the conventional view of the novel takes some knocks. It is not going too far to say that, apart from Reardon, the other main characters are not Milvain, Biffen, and the rest, but houses and streets. It begins to seem something other than an "astute and probing analysis of the 'business' of literature . . ." What it begins to seem is a work primarily concerned with the question of the relationship between man and his whole environment, a work about man and the modern city.

Seeing it in these terms, though, inevitably raises the question of the status of all the minor characters. Just what function are they serving in the novel, beyond being a collection of isolated men in the waste land of London. There is a sense in which nearly all the details of their lives could be sacrificed, and the symbolic force of the novel would remain unimpaired. Indeed, it could be argued that the clumsy derivativeness of their presentation is due to the fact that they are superfluous to the problem Gissing is really exploring. But why then did he not abandon them to produce a more austere, more single-minded, novel? I think it was due to his lack of awareness of just what an original novel he was producing. The novel is moving beyond conventional realism, but Gissing does not seem to be aware of just how powerful his symbolic effects are. So he clings conservatively to conventional characters, even though they are almost irrelevant to the work he was producing. The direction in which the novel is heading is towards the lean integrity of Knut Hamsun's *Hunger*, but Gissing's lack of awareness of his own originality, or possibly his awareness of what novel readers expected, means that some of the force of the novel is dissipated by flaccid character development. But the blundering presentation of minor characters can be overlooked. The novel is a success; but a success, and this is where a formalist approach would come in conflict with a content-based approach, not because of its realistic picture of literary London, but because it turns away from the moral realism of mid-Victorian fiction, to explore a more frightening, more impersonal world, which can only be properly conveyed by a reliance on symbols.

NOTES

1. P.J. Keating, *George Gissing: New Grub Street* (1968), p.9.
2. *New Grub Street* (1891), Penguin edition (1968), p. 35.
3. *Ibid.*, p. 77.
4. Irving Howe, *A World More attractive* New York, 1963), p. 184.
5. *Op. cit.*, pp. 470-71.
6. *Ibid.*, p. 419.
7. *Ibid.*, p. 420.

7

Gissing's *New Grub Street* and "The Triple-Headed Monster"

by JAMES M. KEECH*

To the average Victorian reader of fiction, a novel meant, not the one-volume product of varying length of today, but a fairly standardized set of three post-octavo volumes of about 300 pages per volume. The reader might, of course, have read his novel in the part-issue format used by Dickens or as a serial in a magazine, but these formats he would have regarded as preliminary to publication in volume form. The three-volume novel, or three-decker as it was called, was ultimately the most respectable form for a novel in the nineteenth century.

This average reader would probably have borrowed his novel from a lending library instead of purchasing it; for the three-decker's standard price to the public, 31s. 6d. or the equivalent in purchasing power today of about $35.00, drove the novel-reader from the book stalls to the libraries. There, at a library such as Mudie's Select Library of London, for the small subscription of a guinea a year, he could obtain as recent a volume of fiction as any in the library of a lord. To borrow the complete set of three volumes, however, would have cost him the price of three subscriptions.

Thus existed the highly commercial system for the manufacture of fiction in three volumes. The reader was

* "Gissing's *New Grub Street* and 'The Triple-Headed Monster'" by James Keech: reprinted from *The Serif*, I, 1970, by permission of the editors.

reasonably contented to borrow cheaply rather than buy at great expense; the lending libraries were happy because the high price of novels virtually eliminated outright purchase and created buyers; publishers were happy because with high prices, small editions, and the almost assured purchases of the libraries, the risk involved in publishing was indeed small. Only authors were materially dissatisfied with the three-volume system.

The major difficulty, of course, was length. The three-decker was forbidding in its length, on the average about 168,000 words[1] or about twice the size of Twain's *Huckleberry Finn*. As Anthony Trollope observed in his *Autobiography*, "In writing a novel the author soon becomes aware that a burden of many pages is before him."[2]

Novelists, particularly those with defective imaginations, frequently decried the "Procrustean" length to which they were forced to write. In letters, in diaries, even in the novels themselves one finds their complaints, such as this by Frederic Marryat:

> Should you feel half as tired with reading as I am with writing. I forgive you, with all my heart if you throw down the book and read no more. I have written too fast—I have quite sprained my imagination . . . It's a very awkward position to have to write a chapter of sixteen pages, without materials for more than two; at least I find it so. Some people have the power of spinning out a trifle of matter covering a large surface with a grain of ore—like the gold-beater who out of a single guinea will compose a score of books I wish I could.[3]

George Gissing's *New Grub Street* (3 vols., 1891) offers an interesting insight into the nature of the three-volume systems of publishing fiction, its dependence upon the favour of the lending libraries, and the agony suffered by the type of novelist whose talents were not suited to the system. Jasper Milvain, the soulless journalist, does not attempt a novel, for he realizes it is beyond his facile talents; to him the novel is "a triple-headed monster, sucking the blood of English novelists",[4] and he does not succumb to the lure of financial rewards it offers. All other writers in Gissing's book, however, who attempt the novel are failures. Biffen, who refuses to pander to public taste, receives a paltry £15 for his artistic integrity in *Mr. Bailey, Grocer.* Whelpdale's novels are full of talk and do not sell. Edwin Reardon, however, represents the most tragic example of the three-decker's tyranny.

Reardon's talents are simply unsuited to the novel's format. Unlike the successful writers of three-volume novels, such as Trollope with his *Barchester Towers*, who crowded their pages with a panorama of characters and incidents and thus filled up their pages, Reardon's forte lay with the development of intellectual ideas through psychological analysis of character:

> Those two books of his were not of a kind to win popularity. They dealt with no particular class of society (unless one makes a distinct class of people who have brains), and they lacked local colour. Their interest was almost purely psychological. It was clear the author had no faculty for constructing a story, and that pictures of active life were not to be expected of him; he could never appeal to the multitude.[5]

Such was not the stuff from which successful three-deckers were written, and Reardon's attempts at composition of his last novel are pure agony. He decides "upon a story of the kind natural to him; a 'thin' story, and one which would be difficult to spin into three volumes."[6] He sits at his writing desk for hours, produces only a few threads of sentences, and painfully realizes that each slip of manuscript is a mere fraction of what is needed. The three volumes lie before him "like an interminable desert".

Reardon's solution to his problem was one common to most Victorian novelists: padding. Even Anthony Trollope, the antithesis of the type of novelist represented by Reardon, described the profession of authorship as the "padding trade".[7] Thus it is no surprise to be told that "Reardon's story in itself was weak, and his second volume had to consist almost entirely of laborious padding."[8]

The easiest kind of padding for an author to produce, and the most damaging to the organic integrity of a novel, was dialogue. Characters could be made to patter on about trivia or their own irrelevant interests, and page after page would soon be filled. It was, for the most part, a rather mechanical solution, for a page of dialogue required fewer words than a page of regular narration. If a novelist could shift his speakers rapidly, giving

157

each only a sentence or two to speak, he could fill the page with up to twenty-five per cent fewer words. It was an easy solution, and one Victorian novelists frequently employed, as George Meredith's comments, when working as a publisher's reader testify: "chiefly done by indifferent talk"; "worked out chiefly in flimsy dialogue"; "we have the 3 vols. eked out with sawdust dialogue, in the known manner."[9] Reardon's novel would have evoked from Meredith a similar complaint, for Gissing tells us:

> Description of locality, deliberate analysis of character or motive, demanded far too great an effort for his present condition. He kept as much as possible to dialogue; the space is filled so much more quickly, and at a pinch one can make people talk about the paltriest incidents of life.[10]

In *New Grub Street*, Reardon's novel, of course, is a failure. As Milvain observes, "The misfortune was that you had to make three volumes of it. If I had leave to cut it down to one, it would do you credit."[11] The question raised by Reardon's anguish in producing a book which he knew would be a failure is: why did such an arduous and artificial system for the production of fiction continue to exist when it created such pain and difficulty for the novelist? The answer supplies the complete *raison d'être* of the three-volume system: it was profitable to all concerned. Even Reardon, knowing the damage done by the three-decker to his own creativity, can not abandon the system:

> "For anyone in my position," said Reardon "how is it possible to abandon the three volumes? It is a question of payment. An author of moderate repute may live on a yearly three volume novel—I mean the man who is obliged to sell his book out and out, and who gets from one to two hundred pounds for it. But he would have to produce four one-volume novels to obtain the same income; and I doubt whether he could get so many published within the twelve months. And here comes in the benefit of the libraries; from the commercial point of view the libraries are indispensable. Do you suppose the public would support the present number of novelists if each book had to be purchased? A sudden change to that system would throw three fourths of the novelists out of work."

158

"But there's no reason why the libraries shouldn't circulate novels in one volume."

"Profits would be less, I suppose. People would take the minimum subscription."[12]

Ironically, perhaps, Gissing's novel foreshadows the death of the three-decker system. In contemplating a new novel, Reardon muses:

> ... he saw that he must perforce plan another novel. But this time he was resolute not to undertake three volumes. The advertisements informed him that numbers of authors were abandoning that procrustean system.[13]

The three-volume novel passed away in 1894, when it ceased to be profitable. Through the century the illiteracy rate had been dropping, to five per cent in 1890, establishing a market for the outright sales of novels. A number of novelists like those mentioned in *New Grub Street* had tapped that market in the late 1880s by publishing novels in one volume, such as George Moore's *A Mummer's Wife* (1885), and thus proved the feasibility of mass market sales at lower prices. In addition, more novels than ever appeared in three volumes, reducing the run of popularity of the latest favourite at the libraries and forcing them to purchase more of the short-lived new favourites. When new and aggressive publishing firms began issuing cheap one-volume reprints of novels soon after the expensive first edition the libraries increasingly felt the pinch for profits.

The three-volume system was finally scuttled in June of 1894 when the two great lending libraries of Mudie and W.H. Smith and Sons sent ultimatums to the publishers which were impossible to meet without destroying the economic balance of the system.

The three-decker was replaced by the one-volume novel of today. It had held a long reign, over seventy years, beginning with the highly profitable novels of Sir Walter Scott which had established the fixed format and price. It had created a concept of the novel as a thick panoramic entity, and it had agonized hundreds of novelists who had to fit their talents to a set mould. George Gissing was certainly one of them.

159

It seems quite obvious that Reardon's struggles in *New Grub Street* paralleled Gissing's own difficulties in writing for the three-volume format. He had to write the next-to-last chapter of *Born in Exile* in two days when his manuscript for the third volume was found to be too short.[14] He also admitted in 1901 the "superfluities" in those novels written "when English fiction was subjected to the three volume system".[15] The revisions of these novels for foreign translations support Gissing's admission. *New Grub Street* was shortened by a third in the French translation, and four-fifths of the excised material was dialogue. *The Unclassed*, a three-decker, first published in 1884, was revised as one-volume in 1895, as was *The Emancipated* in 1893. He cut down *Thyrza* (3 vols., 1887) for the six shilling reprint in 1891; and in a letter to Eduard Bertz said that he felt he improved the novel in shortening it.[16]

How many Victorian three volume novels would be improved by removal of the "superfluities"? One is almost tempted to say, with valid justification, all of them. Certainly the insight into the problems of the novelists given by Gissing's *New Grub Street*, the three-decker's immense length and the temptations to pad it into shape, renders all of them suspect. Perhaps the greatest benefit, however, from Gissing's novel would be a sympathetic understanding of why Victorian three-volume novels are occasionally slow in movement, why they seem at times to be interminable, and why some of the dialogue appears to dreadfully inane. With a recognition of the problems a Victorian novelist had to overcome, his accomplishments may appear even greater.

NOTES

1. Charles E. and Edward S. Lauterbach, "The Nineteenth-Century Three-Volume Novel", *Papers of The Bibliographical Society of America*, LI(1957), 285.
2. Anthony Trollope, *An Autobiography* (Berkeley, Calif. 1947), p. 198.
3. *The King's Own*, (London, 1830), II, 255-56.
4. George Gissing, *New Grub Street*, Riverside Ed. (Boston, 1962), p. 168.
5. *Ibid.*, pp. 52-3.

6. *Ibid.*, p. 102.
7. *The Letters of Anthony Trollope*, ed. Bradford A. Booth (London, 1951), p. 85.
8. *New Grub Street*, p. 109.
9. Royal A. Gettmann, *A Victorian Publisher* (Cambridge, 1960), p. 255.
10. *New Grub Street*, p. 103.
11. *Ibid.*, p. 168.
12. *Ibid.*, pp. 168-69.
13. *Ibid.*, p. 133.
14. Gettman, p. 251.
15. *Ibid.*, p. 253.
16. *The Letters of George Gissing to Eduard Bertz 1887-1903*, Arthur C. Young, ed. (New Brunswick, N.J., 1961), p. 120.

8

"The Valley of the Shadow of Books": Alienation in Gissing's *New Grub Street*

by ROBERT L. SELIG*

Gissing's *New Grub Street* (1891) records the estrangement of the writer from the society for which he writes. Pathetically personal and deeply moving though the book is, its broader fascination lies in its vivid account of the profession of letters at a given time. In late-Victorian England marketable goods were more and more produced by machine, leaving the writer a somewhat old-fashioned figure, still creating in the slow way of the past. His isolation from his time was increased by the very nature of his craft, which immersed him in the timeless world of silent print. Perhaps most importantly of all, his transcendental belief in the value of written words estranged him from a world of commerce that tried to reduce all human effort to cash.

A number of admirable studies, both new and old, have commented on *New Grub Street*'s theme of alienation, but briefly, or merely in passing.[1] This study proposes to concentrate on alienation as central to the novel. Although Gissing succeeds, at least partly, in rendering his own estrangement and that of fellow writers in terms of art, the novel also retains undeniable elements of case history. These may lessen its literary distinction, yet they enhance the book's value for cultural

* "The Valley of the Shadow of Books: Alienation in *New Grub Street*" by Robert Selig: reprinted from *Nineteenth Century Fiction*, XXV, 2 September 1970, pp. 188-98, by permission of the editors.

historians. What Gissing said by conscious intent about alienation is illuminating. What he revealed unintentionally, as a deeply involved recorder of writers' lives, illuminates still more. To do justice to this second aspect of his novel, one must combine textual analysis with historical perspectives unavailable to Gissing himself.

If all of Gissing's writers live in a late-Victorian world of large-scale industry and machines, only Milvain, the "Man of his Day",[2] is really enthusiastic about modernity. Two arresting symbols that catch his attention early in the novel reflect the revolution in technology from the eighteenth to the nineteenth century. The novel's "grizzled" exponent of eighteenth-century literature (1:20), hard-working Alfred Yule, is juxtaposed symbolically in Milvain's mind with a "grizzled" horse, the chief form of eighteenth-century transportation: "a poor worn-out beast, all skin and bone, which had presumably been sent here in the hope that a little more labour might still be exacted from it if it were suffered to repose for a few weeks. There were sores upon its back and legs; it stood in a fixed attitude of despondency, just flicking away troublesome flies with its grizzled tail" (1:57). The symbol of the worn-out horse is particularly appropriate for the hack writer, as *hack* is, of course, derived from hackney horses. Significantly, too, the horse appears to Milvain just two pages after he has consciously identified with a newer form of transportation, an express train to London:

> The front of the engine blackened nearer and nearer, coming on with read force and speed. A blinding rush, and there burst against the bridge a great volley of sunlit steam. Milvain and his companion ran to the opposite parapet, but already the whole train had emerged, and in a few seconds it had disappeared round a sharp curve. The leafy branches that grew out over the line swayed violently backwards and forwards in the perturbed air. "If I were ten years younger," said Jasper, laughing, "I should say that was jolly! It enspirits me. It makes me feel eager to go back and plunge into the fight again. (1:54-5)

The London train is an apt symbol for aggressively ambitious

Milvain, a writer from the provinces who achieves success in London by a cynical exploitation of contemporary markets. By the second half of the nineteenth century, not only was the railroad bringing would-be writers to England's commercial and literary capital, but it had to a great extent replaced the horse-drawn post as a means of shipping literature back to the provinces. In a larger sense, then, the London express symbolizes the revolution in the technology of communication which, as Milvain himself notes in chapter I, has helped to make "our Grub Street of to-day . . . a different place" from "Sam Johnson's Grub Street" (1:9).

Yet whatever the attitude of Gissing's writers toward technological change, each must still create his own literary wares by the same slow and laborious method used for centuries. Like Reardon in chapter 4, each must shape his ideas within his private mind and then, in a process often lasting months, must transform them by hand into hundreds of written sheets. Even Milvain, the would-be "steam engine" (3:154), finds that, under unusual pressures, he must labour "with unwonted effort to produce about a page" (2:257). Alfred Yule's daughter, Marian, is so oppressed by literary work that she dreams ironically of a mechanical author to replace the labours of the writer:

> A few days ago her startled eye had caught an advertisement in the newspaper, headed "Literary Machine"; had it then been invented at last, some automaton to supply the place of such poor creatures as herself, to turn out books and articles? Alas! the machine was only one for holding volumes conveniently, that the work of literary manufacture might be physically lightened. But surely before long some Edison would make the true automaton; the problem must be comparatively such a simple one. Only to throw in a given number of old books, and have them reduced, blended, modernised into a single one for to-day's consumption. (1:195)

Marian's vision of a literary machine suggests a basic difference between old and new Grub Street. The writer's trade, which is partly a handicraft, coexisted in Dr. Johnson's time with hundreds of more common handicrafts at all levels of commerce. And if, at the end of his life, Johnson himself witnessed the early stages of industrial revolution, he still wrote for an industry virtually unchanged since Caxton. If the eighteenth-century author wrote his sheets by hand, his fellow craftsmen in printing and publishing cut letter punches by hand, struck them by hand into blank matrices, cast type, composed it, and printed the final pages all entirely by hand. By the time of *New Grub Street*, however, even the printing industry had at last adjusted to machines. From the appearance in 1814 of the first steam printed newspaper to the multiple rotary presses of the late-Victorian period, the printing of newspapers was speeded up nearly a hundredfold. Book publishers adopted machinery more slowly, but they too gradually mechanized their procedures. Other processes besides printing itself were taken over by machine; machinery was developed, for example, for punch cutting, type casting, and composing[3]. But no Edison had yet developed a mechanized author. The human author, who still supplied to publishers their basic raw material, the written word, was changed, in effect, from a craftsman among craftsmen to an isolated anomaly among industrial employees.

Among the many writers in the novel who are struggling to produce, none, significantly, are poets. There are no poets in the book, even though Gissing, as he wrote his early drafts had been reading *Bell's Lives of the Poets*. Poetry appears only as a regretted absence, as something that cannot be created within the deadening confines of Grub Street. "Yes, yes," thinks Reardon of Homer's *Odyssey*," that was not written at so many pages a day, with a workhouse clock clanging its admonition at the poet's ear. How it freshened the soul! How the eyes grew dim with a rare joy in the sounding of those nobly sweet hexameters" (1:229). This late Victorian prose writer looks yearningly back to the Homeric bard, whose poetry was an expression of the whole man rather than a mere literary commodity.

The classical world of Greece and Rome becomes, for Gissing's writers, a lost yet cherished Eden. In the past, Reardon had planned to take his wife to Greece and Rome as the crowning experience of marriage (2:57; 3:74). Later he insists that his trip there as a bachelor was a deeper and more spiritual pleasure than the highest sexual love (3:66). To the almost starving Biffen, Reardon holds out the hope of a voyage to Greece (3:74). In ironic juxtaposition in the very next chapter, Whelpdale tells of nearly having starved to death in the unhomeric modern town of Troy, New York (3:101). The dying classicist Reardon has deliriums of being in Greece but in a final flash of lucidity, declares pathetically that he shall never see it again (3:210-11, 221).

The classical world is exalted by Reardon as the land where the muses were heard. Throughout the novel, the cadence and sound of classical verse are emphasized. Its singing metres bring relief from Grub Street's silent hackwork. Reardon and Biffen discuss "Greek metres as if they lived in a world where the only hunger known could be satisfied by grand or sweet cadences" (1:262). Biffen needs no excuse at all for "murmuring to himself a Greek iambic line" (2:88). The two writer friends are so absorbed in Euripides that they argue about his metrics even on the public streets (3:59, 60, 77). Into the company of the Greek singing school, Reardon is willing to admit a few more recent classics. He refreshes himself from his own belaboured writing with a canto a day from *The Divine Comedy* (2:67). But late Victorian London is no singing school. When Reardon happens to say out loud a few lines from Shakespeare, he is stared at on the street like "a strayed lunatic" (3:7, 8).

This intuitive contrast between the ancient bards and the mute inglorious writers of modern Grub Street seems more understandable in the light of recent studies by Havelock, Ong, and others.[5] Reardon's beloved Homer was an oral poet, united with his non-literate audience in an intensely immediate form of communication that precluded objectivity and detachment. *New Grub Street*'s prose writers work in silent detachment for an audience of silent readers, whom they never meet. Immersing themselves in the writings of others as well as their own, these bookish men of the late nineteenth century absorb and create silently, in mental isolation.

New Grub Street's central symbol for the alienation of the writer is the British Museum Reading-room. In an early draft the opening scene was actually set in the library.[6] In the final version it serves as the central axis around which the characters revolve. It is where they earn a living, all these drudges, surrounded in turn by other solitary drudges. H.J. Chaytor has explained why such a place, where hundreds of readers sit elbow to elbow in silent isolation, could not have existed before print and simplified prose made silent reading a widespread custom: "The reading-room of the British Museum is not divided into sound proof compartments. The habit of silent reading has made such an arrangement unnecessary; but fill the reading-room with medieval readers and the buzz of whispering and muttering would be intolerable."[7]

Because of its effect of alienation, the Reading-room is jokingly described by Milvain and others as "the valley of the shadow of books" (1:22, 25, 31, 60; 2:43). It is described less jokingly by Marian as a desolate limbo for lost souls:

> The fog grew thicker; she looked up at the windows beneath the dome and saw that they were a dusky yellow. Then her eye discerned an official walking along the upper gallery, and in pursuance of her grotesque humour, her mocking misery, she likened him to a black, lost soul, doomed to wander in an eternity of vain research along endless shelves. Or again, the readers who sat here at these radiating lines of desks, what were they but hapless flies caught in a huge web, its nucleus the great circle of the Catalogue? Darker, darker. From the towering wall of volumes seemed to emanate visible motes, intensifying the obscurity; in a moment the book-lined circumference of the room would be but a featureless prison-limit. (1:195-96)

The Museum resembles a prison of lost souls because it puts its readers behind an invisible wall of silence, in mental and spiritual isolation. If Reardon, for one, likes the Reading-room, his acquired taste for it is part of his mental withdrawal: "The Reading-room was his true home: its warmth enwrapped him kindly; the peculiar odour of its atmosphere—at first a cause of headache—grew dear and delightful to him . . . He was a recluse in the midst of millions" (1:105-6). In the silent library even man's most basic drives must be kept quiet and held in check. Thus, although Milvain has seen Marian many times in "the valley of the shadow of books" and has felt her sexual attraction, it is not until he meets her outside that he finds it possible to speak (1:20-1, 30-1). Human beings are usually not talked to by other human beings in this peculiar "valley". They are reached in silence, largely by the dead, through inanimate words on a page. And whatever thoughts each reader draws from the printed word will probably stay within his own mind until he can transfer them to pages of his own making. In Marian's mocking words, each isolated visitor to the library will, in good time, "make new books out of those already existing, that yet newer books might in turn be made out of theirs" (1:194-95).

The invisible wall of silence extends outward to envelop the lives of these library-goers even when they are away. Marian is forced to return, day after day, from the British Museum to a home which her father runs like a branch-office library. Even the eating of dinner, a time for family talk, occurs among the Yules in library-like silence. Until the moment of being called to eat, Alfred Yule stands "on the hearthrug reading an evening paper" (1:161). His frequent custom at the meal itself is to switch from papers to books (2:288). In the very act of eating, he reaches for a volume and proceeds, in front of his masticating wife and daughter, to read silently (1:164-66). Jasper and Dora Milvain, in their household, also partake of the same silent literary meals: "Each had an open book on the table: throughout the meal they exchanged only a few words" (1:58). Perhaps most revealing of all is Reardon's retreat into print after his final loud quarrel with his departing wife: "He sat reading a torn portion of a newspaper, and became quite interested in the report of a commercial meeting in the City, a thing he would never have glanced at under ordinary circumstances" (2:129). Reardon's somnambulistic escape into newsprint parallels his earlier retreat into the enveloping quiet of the Reading-room. For Reardon by choice, for Marian against her will, the human voice is screened out by print.

In spite of all her efforts to break out into a world of live human voices, poor Marian is condemned to remain within silent walls. At the end of the novel she has been forced, against her deepest desires, to become an assistant in a provincial library (3:319). For the still more lonely and isolated Biffen, the Reading-room is not only a place of alienation—it is quite literally "the valley of the shadow of death". When his frustrated desire for a woman's love becomes too much for him, it is from the Reading-room that Biffen gets the recipe for the very efficient poison that will kill him. Even as he goes into the open air to commit suicide first straightening out the books in his room, he remains in silent isolation, for, like the well-trained library-goer that he is, he takes his poison in a deserted park so that he will not disturb the other people who are trying to concentrate in the vast library of the world (3:292-94).

Even when characters do speak in the novel, their words deal very largely with silent print. Their talk tends to be of literature, magazines, and the press. They keynote is sounded in the novel's very first pages with a conversation based on a newspaper story: a criminal is being hanged in London at the moment that Milvain discusses his death. Milvain, who lives and works in the realm of print, can regard a printed description of another's execution as a mere matter of words, to be viewed with detachment. Milvain's remarks about the hanged man lead, in fact, to a discussion of Reardon's professional troubles, his own plans as a writer, and the problems of writers in general (1:1-11). The implied connection is bitterly ironic: getting hanged is an easier way of breaking into print than writing. A similar thought occurs later to Biffen when he is nearly burned to death rescuing his manuscript: "*The Daily Telegraph* would have made a leader out of me. 'This poor man was so strangely deluded as to the value of a novel in manuscript which it appears he had just completed, that he positively sacrificed his life in the endeavour to rescue it from the flames.' And the *Saturday* would have had a column of sneering jocosity on the irrepressibly sanguine temperament of authors. At all events, I should have had my day of fame" (3: 190). For print-oriented men, not only human words but human actions themselves, even those of the most dramatic kind, have no lasting value unless they are translated into the realm of print. In the words of that bookish Renaissance man Samuel Daniel, "What good is like to this,/To do worthy the writing and to write/Worthy the reading, and the world's delight?"[8]

If Gissing's characters tend to refer everything back to the printed word, they tend, with equal insistence, to refer all human actions back to the concept of money. The novel's opening conversation, dealing with the hanging leads to a discussion of the printed word but also of its cash value. Few other novels, in fact, devote so many passages to money. Out of the book's 956 pages, money is directly mentioned on almost half!

Gissing is bitterly aware that the writer's favourite symbol, the printed word, must take a distant second place to society's favourite symbol. If men of letters care most for print, that silent and objectified preserver of human experience, most men prefer cash, that preserver of human labour in silent, objectified coin and bills. "Blessed money! root of all good, until the world invent some saner economy" (1:284). The average man works in order to earn money with which he may buy the necessities of life. Gissing's high-minded men of letters take "no thought of whether . . . [their] toil would be recompensed in coin of the realm" (3:170), yet discover, to their dismay, that man cannot live by words alone. Prose will bring them bread only by being transformed into money. In this necessity, writers are no different from civilization's other craftsmen, such as smiths, barbers, or shoemakers. They differ in believing that the product of their labour is sublimely transcendent in value apart from the cash it earns. Yet "what the devil," asks Milvain, "is there in typography to make everything it deals with sacred?" (1:17). Behind the literary differences of Reardon's psychological realism (1:110-11), Biffen's naturalism (1;264-67), Whelpdale's "chit-chat" (3:232), Yule's pedantic criticism (1:144-45), the Milvain sisters' hackwork for children (1:134-36), and Milvain's own cynical journalism (1:18), Jasper, the account keeper, is able to see the single essence of money.

Most of the writers in Gissing's novel are just as obsessed by money as by literature. Those on their way to success, such as Milvain, are preoccupied with their earnings, and those on their way to failure, such as Yule, are equally preoccupied with what they cannot earn. Money controls the plot of the novel quite as much as literature does. The book's central event is the bequest, through the will of a minor character, of ten thousand pounds to Reardon's wife, five thousand pounds to Marian, and not a pound to Marian's father. The news of the inheritance is so important that it comes three times in the novel to three separate sets of characters (2:250-57; 3:37-41, 68-75, 85-9).

Until the bequest, things have gone badly for most of Gissing's writers. Reardon's marriage has collapsed through lack of money; the somewhat poor Milvain has hesitated to marry an even poorer Marian; and Alfred Yule has yearned in vain for capital to start a literary magazine. The sudden appearance of unearned cash deflects this flow of events. Reardon's wife is saved from poverty, though too late to help her soon-to-die husband. Poor Marian is treated with respect for the first time and even fought over by Milvain and her father, who see her human value hugely enhanced by her five thousand pounds. But when Marian's creditors default on the will, this unexpected second swerve of capital alters once again the lives of all the characters. Milvain breaks his engagement to the disinherited Marian and takes Reardon's widow instead, conveniently wealthy now. Marian is left to support her blind father and wholly dependent mother on a mere fraction of the former legacy. At the novel's end, Marian, her father, Reardon, and even Biffen have been undone by lack of money, but Milvain, Amy, Dora, Maud, and Whelpdale have been rescued by its golden presence.

Of all of Gissing's men of letters, Reardon and Biffen alone are not obsessed by money. They fail, of course, as writers largely through their innocence of all financial realities. A tough-minded attitude toward money undoubtedly helps a writer's career. Yet a mercenary state of mind may conflict, even more than bookishness, with a writer's personal relationships. Such is the case with the cynical Milvain. Although Jasper, unlike Reardon and Biffen lives more for money than for print, the result is a similar alienation, a debilitating isolation from full human contact. "He, too, was weak," Gissing declares of Milvain, "but with quite another kind of weakness than Reardon's" (2:189). The contrast seems to lie in the very different ways that each expresses a similar inadequacy. Reardon withdraws from fellow human beings. Milvain uses them for his own material gain with a cold detachment that leaves him, in effect, as isolated among people as Reardon in solitude. Even when he falls in love with Marian, Milvain cannot put his feelings into speech. "She had looked forward with trembling eagerness to some sudden revelation; but it seemed as if he knew no word of the language which

171

would have called such joyous response from her expectant soul" (2:307). "It was with a sense of relief that Jasper had passed from dithyrambs to conversation on practical points" (2:313-14)."She hid her face against him, and whispered the words that would have enraptured her had they but come from his lips. The young man found it pleasant enough to be worshipped, but he could not reply as she desired. A few phrases of tenderness, and his love-vocabulary was exhausted" (3:115). More, in fact, than Gissing's other writers, Milvain, the man of pounds and shillings, finds it hard to use the spoken word for anything but superficial talk.

There is, perhaps surprisingly, a strong similarity between the supposedly opposite mentalities of literary and economic man. If one wishes to translate everything into print, the other translates everything into money. Both abstractions place human value in frozen, inanimate objects rather than in men. A commonplace figure in nineteenth-century fiction, in Dickens and many others, is the miserly businessman who views all human relationships in terms of mere cash and thus converts even himself into cash both in his own and in others' eyes. Such unlikeminded writers in Gissing's novel as Milvain and Yule accept the creed of the worshipper of cash: a man with money is valued for his money; a man without money is not valued at all. This ironic connection of literary and economic man is underscored by Amy Reardon's shift from one abstract belief to the other. Her first reason for ceasing to love her husband is his failure to produce great books. Later, as she "matures", her chief complaint becomes his failure to earn enough money. Both failures justify, in her view, a total withdrawal of her love (1:90-2, 117, 216, 222; 2:107, 116, 119, 121-22, 139-40). In other words, both economic and literary man, in their extreme forms, are deadening abstractions, which are analogous, mutually illuminating, and even interchangeable. Gissing, in *New Grub Street* has journeyed not only into the shadow of books but also into the shadow of money. Out of this double vision of desolation self-indulgent or not, comes perhaps the finest study in late-Victorian literature of alienation among the people of the book.

NOTES

1. John Gross, "Introduction", *New Grub Street* (London, 1967), pp. v-xii; Jacob Korg, *George Gissing: A Critical Biography* (Seattle, 1963), pp. 154-65; Irving Howe, *A World More Attractive: A View of Modern Literature and Politics* (New York, 1963), pp. 169-91; Bernard Bergonzi, "The Novelist as Hero", *Twentieth Century* 164 (November 1958): 444-55; V.S. Pritchett, "A Chip the Size of a Block", *New Statesman and Nation*, 14 June 1958, p. 781; Mabel Collins Donnelly, *George Gissing: Grave Comedian* (Cambridge, Mass., 1954), pp. 156-61; Q.D. Leavis, "Gissing and the English Novel", *Scrutiny* 7 (June 1938): 73-81.
2. George Gissing, *New Grub Street*, 3 vols. (London, 1891), 1: 1; hereafter referred to in the text by volume and page number.
3. A good account of the mechanization of publishing can be found in Marjorie Plant's *The English Book Trade: An Economic History of the Making and Sale of Books* (London, 1939), especially pp. 274-75, 281-86, 290-97, and 357-59.
4. Diary of George Gissing, II, 4 and 10 June 1890, Berg Collection, New York Public Library, courtesy of Astor, Lenox, and Tilden Foundations.
5. See especially Eric A. Havelock, *Preface to Plato* (Cambridge, Mass., 1963); Walter J. Ong. S.J., *The Presence of the Word: Some Prolegomena for Cultural and Religious History* (New Haven, 1967). Marshall McLuhan's controversial books—*The Gutenberg Galaxy: The Making of Typographic Man* (Toronto, 1962) and *Understanding Media: The Extensions of Man* (New York, 1964)—have done much to popularize studies of this kind.
6. Diary, II, 7 May 1890.
7. H.J. Chaytor, *From Script to Print: An Introduction to Medieval Literature* (Cambridge, 1945), p. 19.
8. Samuel Daniel, "Musophilus", *Poems and a Defense of Ryme*, ed. Arthur Colby Sprague (Cambridge, Mass., 1930), p. 74, lines 198-200.

9

George Gissing (*New Grub Street*)

by JOHN MIDDLETON MURRY*

In *New Grub Street* there is again a perceptible excess of failure. There are in it three "Gissing men"—recognisable aspects or potentialities of himself: Edwin Reardon, Harold Biffen and Alfred Yule. Yule is the scholarly man of letters, who lives by serious and ill-paid journalism, and is compelled to take his wife from behind the counter of a small grocer's shop; Biffen is the down-and-out writer with an ideal, both of a novel to be written and of a woman to be worshipped; Reardon is the actual struggling novelist, who has succeeded in marrying his ideal woman, Amy Reardon. Yule degenerates under the pressure of disappointed ambition and professional jealousy. Biffen dies dreaming that Amy is the perfect woman, when she has in fact failed Reardon. Reardon dies in the illusion that Amy's love for him which has not stood the strain of poverty, is restored. But Amy marries Milvain, the cynical journalist who writes for the market and cultivates society as the means to literary success. He uses his position to establish Reardon's posthumous reputation; she is happy, and the irony is complete.

But it is Reardon who is the central figure of the book. He belongs with Kingcote and Peak; but unlike them, he attains his desire. He does at least marry his ideal woman. Amy and he have been in love; but under the stress of disappointment,

---

* "George Gissing" by John Middleton Murry: an extract reprinted from *Katherine Mansfield and Other Literary Studies* (1959), pp. 15-20, by permission of the editors.

GEORGE GISSING (NEW GRUB STREET)

poverty and anxiety, her love grows cold, and she becomes hard. The effect on Reardon is disastrous, for he depends upon the warmth of his woman's sympathy. His energy as a writer—his inspiration, if you will—fails under his wife's growing estrangement. It is to be remarked, though it is obvious, that Gissing's own energy and inspiration did not fail under similar, but even more grievous, conditions: when the poverty and anxiety were as great, and Amy Reardon's place was occupied by a violent and evil-minded shrew.

It is all beautifully done: particularly, perhaps, in the sense Gissing conveys to us that Amy is ambivalent, that there is in her a potential that might go either way; that she is, as it were, plastic, and if Reardon had had greater determination, and displayed more resolution, she might have stood by him. As it is, confronted by his weakness, at the crucial moment the unregenerate, or purely instinctive, female gets the upper hand. In essence, it is the Kingcote-Isabel situation over again: with a difference. The difference, according to the angle from which it is viewed, is either that Isabel is of finer stuff than Amy, or that Amy is put to the real test, where Isabel is not. Or, in terms of the man, that Reardon has at least the courage to make the trial, where Kingcote shrinks even from that. "I dread the ideal," says Kingcote to his friend Gabriel. Reardon grasps at it, and it wilts at his touch. It becomes a woman of flesh and blood, on whom he has not the strength to impose his purpose or his values.

New Grub Street is a fine novel; probably, with *Born in Exile*, it shares the high distinction of being Gissing's very best. It is not a criticism of Gissing's work, but a fuller understanding of it, that is intended by emphasising the fact that in the three novels in which the hero is recognisably close to a self-portrait, he is consciously or unconsciously drawn to weight the scale of destiny against him. Whether through trick of the man's circumstance or defect of his character, the ideal woman is unattainable, or if attained, turns into something remote from the dream. Lack of money is hardly more than the symbol of a deeper cause of frustration. It is not really operative in Kingcote or in Peak: indeed, in their case, Gissing deliberately designs a final situation of economic security for the man, in order to show that it is not. It would be truer to the impression made by these books to say that the ideal woman is made unattainable by the nature of things, or by some inexorable and hidden law which either forbids fruition or turns it to ashes in the author's imagination.

And in *New Grub Street* Gissing imaginatively explored the consequences of the realisation of his unattainable dream. He was saying to himself: "This is what would happen if the impossible were possible and actual." He is engaged in exorcising the ideal, and in consoling himself that he is better as he is.

The strange and pitiful fact of Gissing's history supplies the key to the mystery. He was—or he was persuaded he was—shut out from the love and companionship he longed for, not by lack of money, but by fear that the scandal of the past would be revealed. By that fear he was inhibited from moving freely in the society which his gifts had opened to him. Still worse, he had been constrained by his hunger for a woman to enter on a second marriage even more disastrous than his first. On September 16, 1890, he wrote in his diary: "I feel like a madman at times. I know I shall never do any more good work till I am married." According to Roberts, his desperation reached such a pitch that he rushed out into the street and spoke to the first accessible woman he met. That, no doubt, is an exaggeration; but substantially it is true. There was no possibility or pretence of rational choice in his second marriage. Even so, the comfort of release from his sexual starvation was such that under its stimulus he worked quickly and well—on *New Grub Street*. The irony of that particular consequence is grim indeed. In it Gissing says of Alfred Yule:

> He could not do without nourishment of some sort, and the time had come when he could not do without a wife. Many a man with brains but no money has been compelled to the same step. Educated girls have a pronounced distaste for London garrets; not one in fifty thousand would share poverty with the brightest genius ever born. Seeing that marriage is so often indispensable to that very success which would enable a man of parts to mate equally, there is nothing for it but to look below one's own level, and to be grateful to the untaught woman who has pity on one's loneliness.

Unfortunately, Alfred Yule was not so grateful as he might

have been. His marriage proved far from unsuccessful; he might have found himself united to a vulgar shrew, whereas the girl had the great virtues of humility and kindliness. She endeavoured to learn of him, but her dullness and his impatience made this attempt a failure; her human qualities had to suffice. And they did, until Yule began to lift his head above the literary mob. . . .

Possibly, for a moment, Gissing had persuaded himself that his new wife, Edith Underwood, had the great virtues of humility and kindness. There is no means of telling; it is not improbable. But she quickly turned out to be a vulgar shrew, and one of the pernicious sort who enchains a man by her sexual attraction. But whether or not Mrs. Alfred Yule embodied Gissing's hopes of his new wife, there is little doubt that while he was writing *New Grub Street* he was comforting his imagination with the thought that a marriage to a social equal would have proved disastrous. For in that book even Amy Reardon, under the pressure of poverty and disappointed ambition, breaks down into the shrew. When Reardon, made desperate by his failure, grasps at a modest clerkship to keep the hounds of anxiety at bay, she coldly refuses to share his poverty. Reardon, overwrought, tries to exert his authority. As his wife, she must do as he thinks fit.

"Do as you think fit? Indeed!"

Could Amy's voice sound like that? Great Heaven! With just such an accent he had heard a wrangling woman retort upon her husband at the street corner. Is there then no essential difference between a woman of this world and one of that? Does the same nature lie beneath such unlike surfaces?

He had but to do one thing: to seize her by the arm, drag her up from the chair, dash her back again with all his force—then the transformation would be complete; they would stand towards each other on the natural footing. With an added curse perhaps—

Instead of that, he choked, struggled for breath, and shed tears.

Amy turned scornfully away from him. Blows and a curse would have overawed her, at all events for the moment. She would have felt: "Yes, he is a man, and I have put my destiny in his hands". His tears moved her to a feeling cruelly exultant; they were a sign of her superiority. It was she who should have wept, and never in her life had she been further from such a display of weakness.

10

Gissing and the English Novel

by Q.D. LEAVIS*

Stories and Sketches by George Gissing (Michael Joseph, 7/6d)

These stories, which mistaken piety must have induced Mr.
A.C. Gissing to publish, will unfortunately persuade no one to
read George Gissing who is not already interested in him. They
exhibit chiefly his weaknesses and give no indication of his
virtues. This is nothing like as interesting a volume of stories as
the better of his other two collections, *The House of Cobwebs*,
which ought by now to have been put into one of the pocket
libraries together with the interesting long "Introductory
Survey" Thomas Seccombe wrote for the 1906 edition. But if
this new volume had persuaded reviewers to look up Gissing's
novels, re-estimate his achievement, and demand for *New Grub
Street* recognition as a classic, its publication would have been
justified. There have been no such signs of a reviewer's
conscience. It is odd that the Gissing vogue—subsequent to the
Meredith vogue and much less widespread—has faded even out
of literary history.

This is discouraging, but let us disinter Gissing nevertheless.
He wrote twenty-two long novels but only one that posterity
would want to read, two books of reminiscence (one the
extremely popular *Private Papers of Henry Ryecroft*), two (now
three) volumes of short stories, and the best existing critical

* "Gissing and the English Novel" by Q.D. Leavis: reprinted from *Scrutiny*
VII, June 1938, pp. 73-81.

introduction to Dickens, in twenty-six years of authorship (he died in 1903 aged only forty-six). He has already received adequate biographical and critical attention in *George Gissing: A Critical Study* by Frank Swinnerton, a capital piece of work which looks like remaining the last profitable word on Gissing as a man and a writer. (Nevertheless academic theses have since been excogitated on the same subject in English, German and American.)

Gissing's life and temperament, with the problems that they raise, are the key to both his many failures and his single success as an artist. He made a false start in life, it is true (a blasted academic career, a spell in prison, a spell in America, an impossible marriage), but on the literary side his sending a copy of his first novel (*Workers of the Dawn*, 1880) to Frederick Harrison resulted much like Crabbe's application to Burke. Harrison recommended Gissing to Lord Morley, then editor of *The Pall Mall Gazette*, and engaged Gissing as classical tutor to his two elder sons, also helping him to get other pupils. He was thus, with the *entrée* to the P.M.G. and as many pupils as he could teach, provided for congenially enough—that is, congenially enough for any other man of letters. But this unfortunate idea of what was suitable for the possessor of literary genius interfered with Harrison's benevolent arrangements. He refused to write more than one sketch for the P.M.G. on the grounds that journalism was degrading work for an artist, and though Mr. Austin Harrison says that from 1882 onwards Gissing had a living income from teaching which he could increase at will, he continued to live, if not actually in cellars and garrets on one meal a day as before, at least in near poverty, because, says Mr. H.G. Wells, "he grudged every moment taken by teaching from his literary purpose, and so taught as little as he could." The interesting point here is not Gissing's romantic conception of what is due to genius, but that he continued to describe himself as the starving and unrecognized martyr of letters; he was for long neither well-to-do nor famous, but Mr. Austin Harrison characterizes his accounts of his "continued struggles with abject poverty" as "fiction of fiction". Gissing apparently needed that fiction to support his self-esteem, his belief in his own genius, for actually he must have been well aware, like his wretched Edwin

Reardon, that he had written mostly what was unworthy of his best abilities. He had to explain his failure by blaming material circumstances; and though his output was really enormous we find him in *Ryecroft*, in the year of his death, picturing himself as the writer obliged to earn his living uncongenially so that he could allow himself, ah but how rarely, the luxury of writing a novel at intervals of many years, and thus was his genius blighted. The facts, as we have seen, were otherwise.

It was not lack of time or means that hampered him, nor yet his unhappy temperament. The latter was perhaps his chief asset, since it produced an absolutely personal way of responding to life and his fellow-men, and when a measure of ultimate success came to (as they say) "mellow" him, the results on his work, as seen in *Ryecroft*, were deplorable. It is instructive to compare the benevolent portrait in *Ryecroft* of the writer N., the successful author and good mixer, with the earlier study of the same type, Jasper Milvain, in *New Grub Street* (when any nineteenth-century novelist names a character Jasper I think we may safely conclude that that character is intended to be the villain). Apart from his temperament all the other qualities he brought to his novels—his scholarship, his bookishness, his enlightened interest in all the leading topics of his day (religious reform, politics, education, emancipation of woman, ethics, science, sociology . . .)—bear witness to his being an exceptionally cultivated man and exceptionally alive in his age, yet apart from *New Grub Street* how those novels date, how unreadable they now are! (It is thus that I seem to hear the literary critic of *Scrutiny*, Vol. L, describing the novels of Mr. Aldous Huxley, whom Gissing in some respects resembles.) But there was no interaction between his subject-matter and his sensibility, so the exhibition of life he gives us seems arbitrarily blighted by a novelist always functioning below par as it were; Mr. Swinnerton, to account for his unpopularity, says "he was condemned by novel-readers as a writer who whimpered at life." But when he took as the subject of a novel his most vital interest—the problem of how to live as a man of letters, the literary world being what it is, without sacrificing your integrity of purpose—he produced his one permanent contribution to the English novel. I think it can be shown to be a major contribution. The subject was both inside and outside him. The best way to suggest his achievement is to say that put beside the other best treatments of the same subject—Maugham's *Cakes and Ale* and the many fine short stories on aspects of the literary life by Henry James which should be read as a whole—Gissing's *New Grub Street* is quite different, equally serious and equally successful as a piece of art.

The Gissing temperament suitably colours the book, which, like *Cakes and Ale* is consistently written in one tone, here an irony weighted with disgust. This strikes one as being the right outlook on the literary world ("such things were enough to make all literature appear a morbid excrescence upon human life", the heroine reflects at one point), if less suited to life in general. However, life in general is here seen from the point of view of the slenderly talented Reardon who wants to support his family by his pen and yet at the same time write only novels and essays worthy of himself. We see him go under, weighed down by a wife who thinks social and material success the due of her beauty, by his lack of influential friends, most of all by his choosing to abide by the values of Dr. Johnson in an age where the policy of Alroy Kear had become requisite for success. We see his acquaintance Jasper Milvain deliberately choosing literature as a profitable field for his unliterary talents and ending up more successful than even he had dared expect, his marriage with Reardon's widow (become an heiress) symbolically ending the story. Delicacy and fineness, the strongly noble and the devotedly disinterested elements in human nature, are not ignored or denied, they are presented with complete success—this is a measure of Gissing's total success here—in the persons of Marian Yule, whom Milvain jilts and leaves to wretchedness, and Reardon's friend Biffen who is driven to remove himself from a world that has no use for his devoted labours. Such are shown doomed to misery and failure. The old-style man of letters, part hack and part stiff-necked enthusiast, is skilfully contrasted (Alfred Yule) with the new-style man of straw (Whelpdale) successful because pliant in his complete lack of any literary conscience. There are many masterly studies of the emotions and conduct peculiar to those who live by literature and journalism, and in spite of a certain stiffness of style from which Gissing was never for long free the smallest touches are effective. The subject seems likely to remain of permanent interest and Gissing has raised crucial problems. The central problem, one ultimately of values, is put by Reardon to his wife thus:

> A year after I have published my last book, I shall be practically forgotten . . . And yet, of course it isn't only for the sake of reputation that one tries to do uncommon work. There's the shrinking from conscious insincerity of workmanship which most writers nowadays seem never to feel. "It's good enough for the market"; that satisfies them. And perhaps they are justified. I can't pretend that I rule my life by absolute ideals; I admit that everything is relative. There is no such thing as goodness or badness, in the absolute sense, of course. Perhaps I am absurdly inconsistent even—though knowing my work can't be first-rate—I strive to make it as good as possible. I don't say this in irony, Amy: I really mean it. It may very well be that I am just as foolish as the people I ridicule for moral and religious superstition. This habit of mine is superstitious. How well I can imagine the answer of some popular novelist if he heard me speak scornfully of his books. "My dear fellow," he might say, "do you suppose I am not aware that my books are rubbish? I know it just as well as you do. But my vocation is to live comfortably. I have a luxurious house, a wife and children who are happy and grateful to me for their happiness. If you choose to live in a garret, and, what's worse, make your wife and children share it with you, that's your concern.

Whether Milvain could have existed at that or any time has, by way of objection, been doubted, but Seccombe, who was in a position to speak with authority, says "Jasper Milvain is, to my thinking, a perfectly fair portrait of an ambitious publicist or journalist of the day—destined by determination, skill, energy and social ambition to become an editor of a successful journal or review, and to lead the life of central London."

It seems to have begun to be as we know it in Gissing's time. Jasper Milvain differs from Alroy Kear (*Cakes and Ale*) only in being a simpler psychological study. Reviewing was much the same as now: "The book met with rather severe treatment in critical columns; it could scarcely be ignored (the safest mode of attack when one's author has no expectant public) . . ." "The struggle for existence among books is nowadays as severe as among men. If a writer has friends connected with the press, it is the plain duty of those friends to do their utmost to help him. What matter if they exaggerate, or even lie? The simple, sober truth has no chance whatever of being listened to, and it's only by volume of shouting that the ear of the public is held." "Literature nowadays is a trade. Putting aside men of genius, who may succeed by mere cosmic force, your successful man of letters is your skilful tradesman. . . . To have money is becoming of more and more importance in a literary career; principally because to have money is to have friends. Year by year, such influence grows of more account . . . Men won't succeed in literature that they may get into society, but will get into society that they may succeed in literature."

The original temper that the novel manifests is notable in every detail, e.g.,

> Alfred Yule had made a rocognizable name among the critical writers of the day; seeing him in the title-lists of a periodical, most people knew what to expect, but not a few forebore the cutting open of the pages he occupied.

> They had had three children; all were happily buried.

> ". . . but I was never snobbish. I care very little about titles; what I look to is intellectual distinction."
> "Combined with financial success."
> "Why, that is what distinction means."

> Amy now looked her years to the full, but her type of beauty, as you know, was independent of youthfulness. You saw that at forty, at fifty, she would be one of the stateliest of dames. When she bent her head towards the person with whom she spoke, it was an act of queenly favour. Her words were uttered with just enough deliberation to give them the value of an opinion; she smiled with a delicious shade of irony; her glance intimated that nothing could be too subtle for her understanding.

The last example is strikingly in the modern manner, and Gissing's best work, *New Grub Street* almost entirely, seems contemporary with us rather than with Meredith.

As a general thing, the same outlook characterizes Gissing's other novels, but elsewhere it seems merely depressed and therefore depressing. Poor Gissing was sliding down the hill which Dickens and his robust contemporaries had climbed in such high spirits. Seccombe explains it well: "In the old race, of which Dickens and Thackeray were representative, a successful determination to rise upon the broad back of popularity coincided with a growing conviction that evil in the real world was steadily diminishing . . ."

In Gissing the misery inherent in the sharp contrasts of modern life was a far more deeply ingrained conviction. He cared little for the remedial aspect of the question. His idea was to analyse this misery as an artist and to express it to the world. One of the most impressive elements in the resulting novels is the witness they bear to prolonged and intense suffering, the suffering of a proud, reserved and oversensitive mind brought into constant contact with the coarse and brutal facts of life. The creator of Mr. Biffen suffers all the torture of "the fastidious, the delicately honourable, the scrupulously high-minded in daily contact with persons of blunt feelings, low ideals and base instincts". Outside *New Grub Street* however you too often feel that the provocation is inadequate to the suffering. Gissing's susceptibilities are not all equally respectable and in some cases he seems only a querulous old maid, too easily provoked on such subjects as bad cooking, slovenly lodgings, ungenteel personal habits and lack of secondary school education. But in *New Grub Street*, just as what is elsewhere merely bookishness becomes transfused into a passionate concern for the state of literature, so his other minor feelings have turned into positive values, and he produced the one important novel in his long list. It occurs less than half-way down, so its unique success is not a matter of maturity or technical development.

The difference between its technical efficiency and the incompetence of the rest is startling too. It might have been written by a Frenchman rather than an Englishman of those days, and Gissing's interest in and admiration for the nineteenth-century Russian and French novelists is significant. He was never able to make use of them as consistently as did Henry James or Conrad but he was conscious that the English novel tradition he had inherited would not do and he was groping for help where it seemed to offer. (He later met Meredith and must have studied *The Egoist* with a certain degree of profit. Literary historians ought to inspect *Our Friend the Charlatan* (1901) which obviously was conceived and treated in the spirit of *The Egoist* though without ceasing to be Gissing's). Gissing is an example of how disastrous it may be for a writer whose talent is not of the first order to be born into a bad tradition. A score and more of novels painfully sweated out of his system, the exceptional system of an exceptionally intelligent and well educated and devoted writer, and only one that amounted to something. The absence of what now enables anyone in Bloomsbury to write a readable novel made Gissing's efforts mostly futile. Mr. Swinnerton justly talks of "the wreckage of the Victorian tradition by which it (Gissing's best work) is now encumbered." But in *New Grub Street* Gissing not only solved, if only temporarily, his own problems, he helped all later writers to solve theirs, and the recognition this novel at one time received from literary men is significant. It is probably an ancestor of the novel of our time.

It is an important link in the line of novels from Jane Austen's to the present which an adult can read at his utmost stretch—as attentively, that is, as good poetry demands to be read—instead of having to make allowances for its being only a novel or written for a certain public or a certain purpose. In the nineteenth century, to take the high lights, Jane Austen, *Wuthering Heights*, *Middlemarch*, *The Egoist*, *New Grub Street* connect the best eighteenth century tradition with the serious twentieth century tradition that Henry James, Conrad, Lawrence, Forster, Joyce and Mrs. Woolf have built up. There are inferior novels (e.g., *The Way of All Flesh*) in this tradition as well as good ones, and very minor successes (like Howard Sturgis's *Belchamber*) as well as major contributions, but they are all immediately recognizable as novels distinct from what we may more usefully call fiction. It is time the history of the English novel was rewritten from the point of view of the twentieth century (it is always seen from the point of view of the mid-nineteenth) just as has been done for the history of English poetry. The student would undoubtedly be glad to be allowed to reorganize his approach and revise the list of novels he has to accept as worth attention; it would be a matter chiefly of leaving out but also of substitution, for the list consists only of conventional values. I don't know who will dare touch off the first charge to blow up those academic values. Mr. Forster once made an attempt on Scott and the response in the academic world was most interesting; the subsequent Scott centenary was a rally of the good men and true to batten down the hatches on Mr. Forster's wholesome efforts to have that reputation reconsidered.

What is commonly accepted as the central tradition is most easily examined in the middling practitioner—such as Trollope or Charles Reade. *The Cloister and the Hearth* is a puerile example of what *Esmond* is a highly accomplished form of, but both are undeserving of serious attention and both are on the educational syllabus, at different ends; though I never knew anyone but the old-fashioned kind of schoolmaster who could bear the former, and the latter's ventriloquial waxworks in period costume (prick them and do they not bleed red paint) are a direct ancestor of Sir Hugh Walpole's own great trilogy which will in time, who can doubt, get on the list too. It is time also that we sorted out the novels which form or enrich the real tradition of the English novel from those which (like Trollope's and Wells's) are rather contributions to the literary history of their time and to be read as material for the sociologist, from those which (like Scott's and R.L.S.'s and George Moore's) perpetrate or perpetuate bogus traditions, from those which (like Charlotte Brontë's) are the ill-used vehicles for expressing a point of view or as in other novelists' hands (Aldous Huxley's), ideas; and from all the other kinds. As one step towards this desirable scheme I suggest that *New Grub Street* be made generally available by reissuing it in "Everyman" or "The World's Classics" editions. Sir Humphrey Milford has already ventured to make some surprising additions to the world's classic novels on his own responsibility (Constance Holmes for instance) and Messrs. Dent have similarly helped Galsworthy and Priestley to get on everyman's list of great novels, so they might do something for Gissing whose best novel will soon be due for a half-centenary.

11

New Grub Street
(Introduction)

by P.J. KEATING*

1

New Grub Street was first published in 1891. It was Gissing's ninth of twenty-two novels, and is easily his most important and enduring work. It holds, however, an unenviable position in the history of the English novel. For although some critics, most notably Q.D. Leavis and Irving Howe, have had no hesitation in proclaiming it a work of art, its continuing interest for the twentieth-century reader lies in Gissing's astute and probing analysis of the "business of literature". First and foremost it is a sociological document; a sociological document of genius written in the form of a novel. Awareness of this point has led Irving Howe to conclude that: "The book is not at all difficult, it is transparent, and to subject it to a 'close reading' in the current academic fashion would be tiresome. What *New Grub Street* asks from the reader is not some feat of analysis, but a considered fullness of response, a readiness to assent to, even if not agree with, its vision and defeat." It is true that an examination of *New Grub Street* for recurrent images and symbolic patterns would not enhance the reader's understanding in the same say as it would with a novel by, say, Dickens, Hardy or Eliot; and it is also true that Gissing's vision

---

* *New Grub Street* (Introduction) by P.J. Keating: reprinted from *Studies in English Literature*, No. 33, 1968, pp. 9-16, by permission of the author.

is one of defeat. But the "considered fullness of response" which is demanded from the reader can only be achieved by a complete awareness of the complexity of the issues being analysed, together with an appreciation of the way in which the author presents his case. Neither the argument nor the presentation of the argument is transparent.

Virginia Woolf pointed out that "Gissing is one of the extremely rare novelists who believes in the power of the mind, who makes his people think", and in *New Grub Street* this quality is of particular importance. Not merely does each character represent certain cultural, social or economic forces, but he is continually made to argue the rights and wrongs of his position. It is as a great debate that *New Grub Street* should be viewed; a debate in which certain key words such as "success", "failure", "popular", "genius", "conscientious", "intellectual", and most of all "practical", recur, developing various shades of irony and ambiguous levels of meaning in such a way that virtually no statement in the book can be taken at face value. Its true meaning will depend on who is speaking, who is being addressed and what stage the debate has reached at that particular moment. The principal speakers fall into three distinct groups; the tradesmen (Milvain and Whelpdale), the artists (Reardon and Biffen) and the men of letters, represented by Alfred Yule. The theme of the debate is the role of literary culture in society, and the central conflict is clearly stated by Milvain in the first chapter:

> But just understand the difference between a man like Reardon and a man like me. He is the old type of unpractical artist; I am the literary man of 1882. He won't make concessions, or rather, he can't make them; he can't supply the market. I—well, you may say that at present I do nothing; but that's a great mistake, I am learning my business. Literature nowadays is a trade.[1]

This, however, is not really the definitive statement it sounds. The basic positions have been established; but the moral, social and cultural issues raised by such an attitude, become clear only when Milvain's bland assumptions are challenged. Is the artist necessarily "unpractical", and what exactly is meant by the word? Is Milvain stating facts, as he appears to be, or is he merely expressing opinions? Is it reasonable to take Reardon as the archetypal artist or would Biffen be a better example? When Milvain talks of supplying the market, does he mean he is satisfying a demand or creating one? These are just a few of the many questions posed by Gissing and to understand the conflicting answers that are given, and the moral crisis that gradually emerges, the allegorical significance of the major characters must be fully explored.

In terms of form there is little in *New Grub Street* to excite attention. Gissing adopted completely the traditional, though by this time fast disappearing, structure of the three-volume novel. The careers of Milvain and Reardon are shadowed by those of Whelpdale and Biffen, who in their minor roles serve both to adumbrate the major issues and to expand the application of those issues to society as a whole. The section dealing with the Yule family is employed as a conventional, though thematically relevant, sub-plot; while control of the action lies firmly in the hands of the ominiscient author, who has no hesitation in addressing the reader in order to point the moral or underline a note of irony.

Yet in spite of the use of this unwieldy novel form ("a tripleheaded monster, sucking the blood of English novelists", as Milvain describes it), *New Grub Street* attains a remarkable degree of unity. This is achieved by a concentration on the careers of a handful of characters, who in their relationships with each other provide a microcosmic view of society. Gissing's method relies heavily on a massive accumulation of detail (intellectual, social, and conversational) which, carefully organised and placed, is used to build up a complex ironic structure. By this means he creates an illusion of having presented to the reader a complete cross-section of the literary life of London. Yet the vicious Fadge, Markland the popular novelist, Jedwood the new type of publisher, the reviewers, the critics, and the society figures who wield such influence, none of the people who dictate the conditions within which the action takes place, ever actually appear in the novel. They exist in a world beyond Reardon's reach; a world to which Milvain goes and returns to report upon. Only in the final chapter do Milvain's influential freinds appear, and then when Reardon is dead and Milvain himself is in a position to be both editor and host. The two worlds are completely incompatible. The success of one entails the annihilation of the other.

Where the two worlds do come together is in their role as guardians of the nation's taste, and they are united in the British Museum Reading-room, which is employed throughout the novel as a symbol of the accumulated knowledge of mankind. Milvain describes Alfred and Marian Yule as "obvious dwellers in the valley of the shadow of books", and his flowery remark anticipates the moment when Marian, gazing up at the Reading-room dome sees herself and the other researchers as "hapless flies caught in a huge web, its nucleus the great circle of the Catalogue". Reardon's response is totally different. He looks back upon his early days in London and remembers the Reading-room as "his true home", and when the drudgery of his three-volume novel is over he relaxes in the Museum, indulging his love of the classics by writing essays on esoteric literary themes. In Chapter VII the Reading-room is seen as a place of lost causes and sterile academic work. Mr. Hinks presents Marian with a copy of his "Essay on the Historical Drama" for her father; and Mr. Quarmby passes on his private information that Alfred Yule is at last to be offered the editorship he longs for—the gossip is as worthless as the book. The courtship between Marian and Milvain is conducted largely from the British Museum; he hurriedly consulting encyclopaedias and she dreaming of the day when a machine will be invented to take over her thankless task. Finally the Reading-room is the place where all illusions are shattered. Alfred Yule refuses to discuss his coming blindness with his daughter, dismissing her with: "You can read up the subject for yourself at the British Museum." And when Biffen plans to poison himself it is to the Reading-room he goes for the necessary knowledge.

This symbolic use of the British Museum is extremely successful but in the main Gissing did not feel at home with symbolism. Nothing could be more crude, for instance, than the moment in Chapter III when Milvain asks Marian to indulge him in a spot of "childishness" and go to watch the London express rush under a bridge. This experience is meant to symbolize both his driving ambition and the disconcerting sexual attraction Marian possesses for him; but the symbol is local and is not integrated into the novel. It is unnecessary and thus distracting. On the other hand, symbolic images, such as the hanged man or the worn-out horse, grow and develop as the novel progresses, heightening the moral uncertainty of a rapidly changing society. In this instance, as in all others, Gissing's craftsmanship is uneven, and his weaknesses should be acknowledged. His writing is at times ponderous and artificially literary and suffers from all of the faults he notes in Reardon's work and some of those in Alfred Yule's. Further, he often seriously underestimates the intelligence of the reader (a significant fault in the author of a book such as *New Grub Street*), and insists on too heavily underlining the motives and emotions of the characters. His sense of humour is best described in the same terms that Biffen uses to excuse Reardon's feeble riddle: "It'll pass. Distinctly professional though. The general public would fail to see the point."

He was a morbidly autobiographical novelist and this has, perhaps, prevented his best work from receiving the critical attention it deserves. Gissing's greatest admirers have often been so busy sifting the novels for biographical analogies that the work itself has been ignored. This is particularly true of *New Grub Street* and is a tendency which should be resisted. Sometimes, as in the portrait of Reardon, Gissing becomes too personally involved and this is a flaw which needs to be recognised, but, in this novel at least, Gissing usually succeeds in distancing himself from the action, and his own attitudes should be judged only when the total pattern of the work has been considered.

2

In terms of subject matter *New Grub Street* is virtually unique. Novels about novelists there have been in plenty but they tend either to concentrate on aspects of the novelist's life other than his writing; or they deal intimately with the growth of a single mind or sensibility. If one compares, for example, *David Copperfield* (1850) and *Pendennis* (1850) on the one hand, *Portrait of the Artist as a Young Man* (1916) on the other, the change in treatment is astounding. Neither David Copperfield nor Arthur Pendennis seem to feel that being a writer is anything to make much of a fuss about.[2] It is a profession which can bring both financial rewards and a place in society. It demands talent and a degree of worldly experience, but not creative agony. Such an attitude is meaningless to Stephen Dedalus. Society is something to escape from, and the very thought that one's work might bring public acclamation is enough to brand one as an inferior artist. The period of Gissing's life (1857-1903) coincides almost exactly with the most important phase of this complex revolution, and historically it is significant that the work nearest in tone to *New Grub Street* is the group of short stories on literary themes written by Henry James in the early 1890s.

The redevance of the title *New Grub Street* is primarily historical. There are several exact comparisons (principally with reference to the work of Reardon and Alfred Yule) but Gissing usually employs the phrase *Grub Street* in either a vaguely emotional or pejorative sense, or to establish an historical frame of reference. That he was fully aware of the various shades of meaning that surround the phrase is made clear in a letter he wrote to his German friend Eduard Bertz on the 26th April, 1891. He writes: "*Grub Street* actually existed in London some hundred and fifty years ago. In Pope and his contemporaries the name has become synonymous for wretched-authordom. In Hogarth's 'Distressed Author' there is '*Grub Street*' somewhere inscribed. Poverty and meanness of spirit being naturally associated, the street came to denote an abode, not merely of poor, but of insignificant, writers." He goes on to quote Dr. Johnson's famous definition: "Originally the name of a street near Moorfields in London, much inhabited by writers of small histories, dictionaries, and temporary poems; whence any mean production is called *grubstreet*." Later in the same letter Gissing says: "At present the word is used contemptuously. You know that I do not altogether mean that in the title of my book."

On one level Gissing is indicating that late Victorian England has created a Grub Street as pernicious as that which existed in the early eighteenth century. Many of the central issues such as the power of the publishers, the suffering and poverty of the authors, the hack-writing of the journalists, the virtual impossibility for anyone—save a genius—to rise out of Grub Street once he is there, the superabundance of mediocre work being churned out for an audience forever demanding more of the same—all this and more is relevant to both periods.

But on another level Gissing is implying that *New* Grub Street is in many ways a logical development of the old. They are not two isolated periods, but both parts of a process of change (what Raymond Williams has called "The Long Revolution") which will lead ultimately to a culturally fragmentated society. The chief historical fact Gissing has in mind when he refers back to the early eighteenth century is the rise of a large commercial middle class, together with the corresponding development of newspapers, the novel and the periodical. These are, of course, the very literary forms with which *New Grub Street* is concerned and each is shown to have suffered, in the process of time, fearful corruption. Jasper Milvain is the modern equivalent of Addison or Steele; Alfred Yule is surely Dr. Johnson; and a popular novelist such as Richardson has become Markland. Characters such as Whelpdale, Fadge and Jedwood are the eternal vampires feeding, consciously or unconsciously, on the blood of struggling writers. This last comparison pinpoints more exactly Gissing's personal attitude to Grub Street, for in some ways he is indulging in a spot of myth-making. It is believed by everyone in *New Grub Street* that genius, true, unadulterated genius, will either rise out of the mire and receive its just acclaim or will suffocate and die scornful of all material reward. Given the social conditions it is more natural that the latter will occur, but genius is *sui generis* and it could just as easily follow the former course. Whatever eventually happens, however, the possessor of genius will, at first, be forced to join the writers in Grub Street. He is not a hack himself but he must rise from the ranks of the hacks, or rather, dwell with them by necessity. Milvain expresses the accepted view: "I am speaking of men who wish to win reputation before they are toothless. Of course if your work is strong, and you can afford to wait, the probability is that half a dozen people will at last begin to shout that you have been monstrously neglected, as you have."

A further analogy being made between the two Grub Streets is the use made of literature to advance personal squabbles and vendettas. "To assail an author without increasing the number of his readers is the perfection of journalistic skill", writes Gissing, and everyone, whether tradesman, artist or man of letters, enjoys a good literary slanging match. When Fadge's

193

periodical, *The Study*, publishes two conflicting reviews of the same novel, Alfred Yule is delighted because the error confirms their totally different views of the market, and even Biffen raises a chuckle.

The main issues examined by Gissing have all become commonplaces of twentieth-century critical thought and discussion. The alienation of the artist from society; the development of a new kind of popular press; an increasingly centralised society dominated by London; the new concept of the art of fiction; and the conscious acceptance by everyone involved of the intellectual, commercial and cultural division of English life. In Chapter XXIX Alfred Yule sums up the situation in a suitably pedantic manner:

> How much better "a man of letters" than "a literary man"! And apropos of that, when was the word "literature" first used in our modern sense to signify a body of writing? In Johnson's day it was pretty much the equivalent of our "culture". You remember his saying, "It is surprising how little literature people have." His dictionary, I believe, defines the word as "learning, skill in letters"—nothing else.

It is the forces making for this change that Gissing sets out to analyse and in doing so brilliantly captures a crucial moment in a period of cultural crisis.

12

George Gissing

by GEORGE ORWELL*

In the shadow of the atomic bomb it is not easy to talk confidently about progress. However, if it can be assumed that we are not going to be blown to pieces in about ten years' time, there are many reasons, and George Gissing's novels are among them, for thinking that the present age is a good deal better than the last one. If Gissing were still alive he would be younger than Bernard Shaw, and yet already the London of which he wrote seems almost as distant as that of Dickens. It is the fog-bound, gas-lit London of the 'eighties, a city of drunken puritans, where clothes, architecture and furniture had reached their rock-bottom of ugliness, and where it was almost normal for a working-class family of ten persons to inhabit a single room. On the whole Gissing does not write of the worst depths of poverty, but one can hardly read his descriptions of lower-middle class life, so obviously truthful in their dreariness, without feeling that we have improved perceptibly on that black-coated, money-ruled world of only sixty years ago.

Everything of Gissing's—except perhaps one or two books written towards the end of his life—contains memorable passages, and anyone who is making his acquaintance for the first time might do worse than start with *In the Year of Jubilee*. It was rather a pity, however, to use up paper in reprinting two of his minor works[2] when the books by which he ought to be remembered are and have been for years completely unprocurable. *The Odd Women*, for instance, is about as

* "George Gissing" by George Orwell: reprinted from the *London Magazine*, June 1960, pp. 36-43, by permission of the editors.

thoroughly out of print as a book can be. I possess a copy myself, in one of those nasty little red-covered cheap editions that flourished before the 1914 war, but that is the only copy I have ever seen or heard of. *New Grub Street*, Gissing's masterpiece, I have never succeeded in buying. When I have read it, it has been in soup-stained copies borrowed from public lending libraries: so also with *Demos*, *The Nether World* and one or two others. So far as I know only *The Private Papers of Henry Ryecroft*, the book on Dickens, and *A Life's Morning*, have been in print at all recently. However, the two now reprinted are well worth reading, especially *In the Year of Jubilee*, which is the more sordid and therefore the more characteristic.

In his introduction Mr. William Plomer remarks "that generally speaking, Gissing's novels are about money and women", and Miss Myfanwy Evans says something very similar in introducing *The Whirlpool*. One might, I think, widen the definition and say that Gissing's novels are a protest against the form of self-torture that goes by the name of respectability. Gissing was a bookish, perhaps over-civilized man, in love with classical antiquity, who found himself trapped in a cold, smoky, Protestant country where it was impossible to be comfortable without a thick padding of money between yourself and the outer world. Behind his rage and querulousness there lay a perception that the horrors of life in late-Victorian England were largely unnecessary. The grime, the stupidity, the ugliness, the sex-starvation, the furtive debauchery, the vulgarity, the bad manners, the censoriousness—these things were unnecessary, since the puritanism of which they were a relic no longer upheld the structure of society. People who might, without becoming less efficient, have been reasonably happy chose instead to be miserable, inventing senseless tabus with which to terrify themselves. Money was a nuisance not merely because without it you starved; what was more important was that unless you had quite a lot of it—£300 a year, say—society would not allow you to live gracefully or even peacefully. Women were a nuisance because even more than men they were the believers in tabus, still enslaved to respectability even when they had offended against it. Money and women were therefore the two instruments through which society avenged itself on the courageous and the intelligent.

196

Gissing would have liked a little more money for himself and some others, but he was not much interested in what we should now call social justice. He did not admire the working class as such, and he did not believe in democracy. He wanted to speak not for the multitude, but for the exceptional man, the sensitive man, isolated among barbarians.

In *The Odd Women* there is not a single major character whose life is not ruined by having too little money, or by getting it too late in life, or by the pressure of social conventions which are obviously absurd but which cannot be questioned. An elderly spinster crowns a useless life by taking to drink; a pretty young girl marries a man old enough to be her father; a struggling schoolmaster puts off marrying his sweetheart until both of them are middle-aged and withered; a good-natured man is nagged to death by his wife; an exceptionally intelligent, spirited man misses his chance to make an adventurous marriage and relapses into futility; in each case the ultimate reason for the disaster lies in obeying the accepted social code, or in not having enough money to circumvent it. In *A Life's Morning* an honest and gifted man meets with ruin and death because it is impossible to walk about a big town with no hat on. His hat is blown out of the window when he is travelling in the train, and as he had not enough money to buy another, he misappropriates some money belonging to his employer, which sets going a series of disasters. This is an interesting example of the changes in outlook that can suddenly make an all-powerful tabu seem ridiculous. Today, if you had somehow contrived to lose your trousers, you would probably embezzle money rather than walk about in your underpants. In the 'eighties the necessity would have seemed equally strong in the case of a hat. Even thirty or forty years ago, indeed, bare-headed men were booed at in the street. Then, for no very clear reason, hatlessness became respectable, and today the particular tragedy described by Gissing—entirely plausible in its context—would be quite impossible.

The most impressive of Gissing's books is *New Grub Street*. To a professional writer it is also an upsetting and demoralizing book, because it deals among other things with that much-dreaded occupational disease, sterility. No doubt the number of writers who suddenly lose the power to write is not large, but it is a calamity that *might* happen to anybody at any moment, like sexual impotence. Gissing, of course, links it up with his habitual themes—money, the pressure of the social code, and the stupidity of women.

Edwin Reardon, a young novelist—he has just deserted a clerkship after a fluky success with a single novel—marries a charming and apparently intelligent young woman, with a small income of her own. Here, and in one or two other places, Gissing makes what now seems the curious remark that it is difficult for an educated man who is not rich to get married. Reardon brings it off, but his less successful friend, who lives in an attic and supports himself by illpaid tutoring jobs, has to accept celibacy as a matter of course. If he did succeed in finding himself a wife, we are told, it could only be an uneducated girl from the slums. Women of refinement and sensibility will not face poverty. And here one notices again the deep difference between that day and our own. Doubtless Gissing is right in implying all through his books that intelligent women are very rare animals; and if one wants to marry a woman who is intelligent *and* pretty, then the choice is still further restricted, according to a well-known arithmetical rule. It is like being allowed to choose only among albinos, and left-handed albinos at that. But what comes out in Gissing's treatment of his odious heroine, and of certain others among his women, is that at that date the idea of delicacy, refinement, even intelligence, in the case of a woman, was hardly separable from the idea of superior social status and expensive physical surroundings. The sort of woman whom a writer would want to marry was also the sort of woman who would shrink from living in an attic. When Gissing wrote *New Grub Street* that was probably true, and it could, I think, be justly claimed it is not true today.

Almost as soon as Reardon is married it becomes apparent that his wife is merely a silly snob, the kind of woman in whom "artistic tastes" are no more than a cover for social competitiveness. In marrying a novelist she has thought to marry someone who will rapidly become famous and shed reflected glory upon herself. Reardon is a studious, retiring, ineffectual man, a typical Gissing hero. He has been caught up in an expensive, pretentious world in which he knows he will never be able to maintain himself, and his nerve fails almost immediately. His wife, of course, has not the faintest understanding of what is meant by literary creation. There is a terrible passage—terrible, at least, to anyone who earns his living by writing—in which she calculates the number of pages that it would be possible to write in a day, and hence the number of novels that her husband may be expected to produce in a year—with the reflection that really it is not a very laborious profession. Meanwhile Reardon has been stricken dumb. Day after day he sits at his desk; nothing happens, nothing comes. Finally, in panic, he manufactures a piece of rubbish; his publisher, because Reardon's previous book had been successful, dubiously accepts it. Thereafter he is unable to produce anything that even looks as if it might be printable. He is finished.

The desolating thing is that if only he could get back to his clerkship and his bachelorhood, he would be all right. The hard-boiled journalist who finally marries Reardon's widow sums him up accurately by saying that he is the kind of man who, if left to himself, would write a fairly good book every two years. But, of course, he is not left to himself. He cannot revert to his old profession, and he cannot simply settle down to live on his wife's money: public opinion, operating through his wife, harries him into impotence and finally into the grave. Most of the other literary characters in the book are not much more fortunate, and the troubles that beset them are still very much the same today. But at least it is unlikely that the book's central disaster should now happen in quite that way or for quite those reasons. The chances are that Reardon's wife would be less of a fool, and that he would have fewer scruples about walking out on her if she made life intolerable for him. A woman of rather similar type turns up in *The Whirlpool* in the person of Alma Frothingham. By contrast there are the three Miss Frenches in *In the Year of Jubilee*, who represent the emerging lower-middle class—a class which, according to Gissing, was getting hold of money and power which it was not fitted to use—and who are quite surprisingly coarse, rowdy, shrewish and unmoral. At first sight Gissing's "ladylike" and "unladylike" women seem to be different and even opposite kinds of animal, and this seems to invalidate his implied condemnation of the female sex in general. The connecting link between them, however, is that all of them are miserably limited in outlook. Even the clever and spirited ones, like Rhoda in *The Odd Women* (an interesting early specimen of the New Woman), cannot think in terms of generalities, and cannot get away from readymade standards. In his heart Gissing seems to feel that women are natural inferiors. He wants them to be better educated, but on the other hand, he does not want them to have freedom, which they are certain to misuse. On the whole the best women in his books are the self-effacing, home-keeping ones.

There are several of Gissing's books that I have never read, because I have never been able to get hold of them, and these unfortunately include *Born in Exile*, which is said by some people to be his best book. But merely on the strength of *New Grub Street*, *Demos* and *The Odd Women* I am ready to maintain that England has produced very few better novelists. This perhaps sounds like a rash statement until one stops to consider what is meant by a novel. The word "Novel" is commonly used to cover almost any kind of story—*The Golden Asse*, *Anna Karenina*, *Don Quixote*, *The Improvisatore*, *Madame Bovary*, *King Solomon's Mines* or anything else you like—but it also has a narrower sense in which it means something hardly existing before the nineteenth century and flourishing chiefly in Russia and France. A novel, in this sense, is a story which attempts to describe credible human beings, and—without necessarily using the technique of naturalism—to show them acting on everyday motives and not merely undergoing strings of improbable adventures. A true novel, sticking to this definition, will also contain at least two characters, probably more, who are described from the inside and on the same level of probability—which, in effect, rules out the novels written in the first person. If one accepts this definition, it becomes apparent that the novel is not an art-form in which England has excelled. The writers commonly paraded as "great English novelists" have a way of turning out either to be not true novelists, or not to be Englishmen. Gissing was not a writer of picaresque tales, or burlesques, or comedies, or political tracts: he was interested in individual human beings, and the fact that he can deal sympathetically with several different sets of motives, and make a credible story out of the collision between

200

them, makes him exceptional among English writers.

Certainly there is not much of what is usually called beauty, not much lyricism, in the situations and characters that he chooses to imagine, and still less in the texture of his writing. His prose, indeed is often disgusting. Here are a couple of samples

"Not with impunity could her thought accustom itself to stray in regions forbidden, how firm soever her resolve to hold bodily aloof." (*The Whirlpool*)

"The ineptitude of uneducated English women in all that relates to their attire is a fact that it boots not to enlarge upon." (*In the Year of Jubilee*)

However, he does not commit the faults that really matter. It is always clear what he means, he never "writes for effect", he knows how to keep the balance between *récit* and dialogue and how to make dialogue sound probable while not contrasting too sharply with the prose that surrounds it. A much more serious fault than his inelegant manner of writing is the smallness of his range of experience. He is only acquainted with a few strata of society, and, in spite of his vivid understanding of the pressure of circumstance on character, does not seem to have much grasp of political or economic forces. In a mild way his outlook is reactionary, from lack of foresight rather than from ill-will. Having been obliged to live among them, he regarded the working class as savages, and in saying so he was merely being intellectually honest; he did not see that they were capable of becoming civilized if given slightly better opportunities. But, after all, what one demands from a novelist is not prophecy, and part of the charm of Gissing is that he belongs unmistakably to his own time, although his time treated him badly.

The English writer nearest to Gissing always seems to be his contemporary, or near-contemporary, Mark Rutherford. If one simply tabulates their outstanding qualities, the two men appear to be very different. Mark Rutherford was a less prolific writer than Gissing, he was less definitely a novelist, he wrote much better prose, his books belong less recognizably to any particular time, and he was in outlook a social reformer and, above all, a puritan. Yet there is a sort of haunting resemblance, probably explained by the fact that both men lack that curse of

English writers, a "sense of humour". A certain low-spiritedness, and air of loneliness, is common to both of them. There are, of course, funny passages in Gissing's books but he is not chiefly concerned with getting a laugh—above all, he has no impulse towards burlesque. He treats all his major characters more or less seriously, and with at least an attempt at sympathy. Any novel will inevitably contain minor characters who are mere grotesques or who are observed in a purely hostile spirit, but there is such a thing as impartiality, and Gissing is more capable of it than the great majority of English writers. It is a point in his favour that he had no very strong moral purpose. He had, of course, a deep loathing of the ugliness, emptiness and cruelty of the society he lived in, but he was concerned to describe it rather than to change it.There is usually no one in his books who can be pointed to as the villain, and even when there is a villain he is not punished. In his treatment of sexual matters Gissing is surprisingly frank, considering the time at which he was writing. It is not that he writes pornography or expresses approval of sexual promiscuity, but simply that he is willing to face the facts. The unwritten law of English fiction, the law that the hero as well as the heroine of a novel should be virgin when married, is disregarded in his books, almost for the first time since Fielding.

Like most English writers subsequent to the mid-nineteenth century, Gissing could not imagine any desirable destiny other than being a writer or a gentleman of leisure. The dichotomy between the intellectual and the lowbrow already existed, and a person capable of writing a serious novel could no longer picture himself as fully satisfied with the life of a business-man, or a soldier, or a politician, or what-not. Gissing did not, at least consciously, even want to be the kind of writer that he was. His ideal, a rather melancholy one, was to have a moderate private income and live in a small comfortable house in the country, preferably unmarried, where he could wallow in books, especially the Greek and Latin classics. He might perhaps have realized this ideal if he had not managed to get himself into prison immediately after winning an Oxford scholarship: as it was he spent his life in what appeared to him to be hackwork, and when he had at last reached the point where he could stop writing against the clock, he died almost immediately, aged

GEORGE GISSING

only about forty-five. His death, described by H.G. Wells in his *Experiment in Autobiography*, was of a piece with his life. The twenty novels, or thereabouts, that he produced between 1880 and 1900 were, so to speak, sweated out of him during his struggle towards a leisure which he never enjoyed and which he might not have used to good advantage if he had had it: for it is difficult to believe that his temperament really fitted him for a life of scholarly research. Perhaps the natural pull of his gifts would in any case have drawn him towards novel-writing sooner or later. If not, we must be thankful for the piece of youthful folly which turned him aside from a comfortable middle-class career and forced him to become the chronicler of vulgarity, squalor and failure.

NOTES

1. This article was originally commissioned for a magazine which came to an end before it could be published. It has only recently come to light again.
2. *In the Year of Jubilee*\and *The Whirlpool* (Watergate Classics).

13

Names in *New Grub Street*

by J.P. MICHAUX

By the time Gissing wrote *New Grub Street* it had been a steady practice among writers to use (for their characters) patronymic appellations which carried with them a clear meaning, thus opening the way for the reader's or listener's interpretation. The custom dates back to the Middle Ages with the emergence of the mystery-plays the meaning of which had to be made clear to each and every spectator. It was a widespread practice as far as Elizabethan plays were concerned—such names as Luxurioso, Spurioso or Vincentio were indicative of what functions the *dramatis personae* would carry out. One can link to this practice the theory of humours and the role played by foils which were good means to illustrate the author's thesis.

Apropos of *New Grub Street* it may be worthwhile to try and see whether Gissing like his master Dickens, still made use of those convenient "labels", so to speak, though it was often less obvious than with his predecessors and even sometimes seemed rather *recherché*.

Reardon: The first part of the name of the flawed novelist is composed of the word "rear", suggesting that he is somewhat past it or that he is behind the times. He seems to belong to the rearguard of the literary world of *New Grub Street*. Reardon is a foil to Milvain who is a promising careerist belonging to the vanguard, not of an intellectual élite but rather of those who profess that literature is becoming a trade. Thus the military terms are well in keeping with the struggle for survival in the

204

literary jungle of *New Grub Street*. Reardon is also in the rear in the sense that he dreams of the good old days of Dr. Johnson, a time when one could live by one's pen. He fails because he cannot advance or come to the fore; in other words he is unable to adapt to changing ethics. It is no wonder then that Amy will leave him and eventually marry Jasper of the facile pen.

The second part of his name, "don" is a profession which Reardon could well have exercised under better circumstances. Everyone agrees that he is a scholar more fit to write essays about Diogenes Laertius or to talk about Greek metres than for the writing of novels (especially three-deckers), which is a drudge to him. As for his Christian name Edwin, the second syllable stands in ironical contrast with his final failure. Reardon then has been hoodwinked by his ideal of classical scholarship throughout the novel. This ideal has made him blind to the harsh reality of commercial success and Jasper Milvain says of him that he "is absurd enough to be conscientious".

Milvain: The first part of his name sounds phonetically the same as mill, a word implying that he is associated with the industrial world which Gissing does not hold in great esteem. Hence the type of work Milvain produces is of a mechanical quality, something made to order or rather according to the well-established law of supply and demand. Milvain himself gives a definition of what his works consist of. Being a success seems to him something which is as automatic as a piece of machinery can be. All he has to do is to follow some recipes: writing according to fashion and public taste ("We people of brains are justified in supplying the mob with the food it likes"), flattering the mass of half-educated readers, or again striking a friendship with influential people. Mr. Bergonzi[1] aptly said that Milvain today "would be clearly destined for a job in advertising or public relations". This seems to emphasize the fact that Milvain undoubtedly has a turn for business, an enterprising spirit. He examines literature coolly and sees in it all types of marketable commodities. Now a mill can also be a pugilistic encounter, and there is no doubt that here again is underlined the Darwinian theory of adaptability of the survival of the fittest: Milvain loses no opportunity and he sacrifices Marian's love to reach his goal. Though he is not depicted as the total villain, yet we may feel sure that he will make his way even if that means trampling others *en route* ("I shall do many a base thing in life, just to get money and reputation; I tell you this that you mayn't be surprised if anything of that kind comes to yours ears"). This aspect of the character is alluded to by Mrs. Leavis who said: "When any nineteenth-century novelist names a character Jasper I think we may safely conclude that that character is intended to be the villain".[2]

"Vain", the second syllable of Milvain, seems to imply that his work will be unavailing, that it is doomed to perish very soon. True he is the first one to acknowledge this. Contrary to Reardon, who would like to achieve great fame through laborious hack-work, Milvain wants to achieve a reputation here-and-now, which is in tune with his ability to write quickly and easily on any subject ("It is my business to know something about every subject—or to know where to get the knowledge"). Conversely Reardon needs time to polish his style and do his best. Vain is also Jasper's career as it only tends towards worldly ends. Now Jasper resembles the French *j'aspire* (= I aspire) and there is no doubt about Milvain's aspirations, so the similarity Jasper/*J'aspire* may not be so far-fetched as it first seems, all the more so as Gissing could speak French. Whether conscious, unconscious or just accidental the fact remains and the association of terms is tempting if not wholly credible.

Amy: Amy does not prove to be the ideal *Ami*(e) or companion Reardon wished her to be (not the Mimi or Musette of Murger's *Scènes de la vie de Bohème* anyway). In all circumstances her love does not bear the test of hardship. She first becomes cold towards her husband, who complains about it. Gradually their relationship deteriorates as Reardon's inability to write his *quantum* of pages and to produce anything becomes obvious. A climax is reached when Reardon discloses his intention to resume his job as a clerk. Amy then is definitely not the *Ame-soeur* (twin-soul) that her husband dreamt about. The dichotomy Amy/*Ami* is ironical in that she eventually becomes Reardon's enemy and even Biffen's as she is the instrument of their deaths, thus playing the role of a kind of vamp for both of them.

Marian's name is almost transparent. She is a kind of Mary, the Virgin mother, if one may venture the comparison. She has numerous qualities: she is knowledgeable and intelligent. Marian can do a lot of work for her father who trusts her to do many things for him. But as Mary she also suffers: first, her hope of a substantial inheritance is blighted; secondly, her love for Jasper is thwarted and the latter rejects her, preferring to marry Amy Reardon, who benefits from a bigger portion of the Yule inheritance. Thus, after suffering from poverty, an overbearing father and the distaste of hackwork, she ends as a librarian in the country (in the end, unable to escape the world of books altogether). In spite of her good intentions she eventually leads a life poles apart from that of Milvain and Amy, and her doom serves as a good example of the importance of money.

Biffen is the hack-writer who is defeated by fate or receives a smart blow, a biff. It is due no so much to the commercial failure of his realistic novel *Mr. Bailey, Grocer*, as to his realization that he cannot escape the sexual urge. His encounter with Amy is the last straw on the camel's back because he cannot help idealizing her. Amy proves the bane of his life and drives him to commit suicide, quoting Shakespeare's famous phrase from *The Tempest* "We are such stuff as dreams are made on." His suicide is all the more unexpected as he is one who is only happy as long as he can get on with his book. He seems indestructible, indifferent to the slings and arrows of his miserable existence. Content to feed himself on bread and dripping, he is yet always ready to cheer up his friend Reardon.

Whelpdale is also a Grub Street dweller and an inveterate skirt-chaser. He is described as a man who cannot resist a woman's charm. Always madly in love with women, he seems to behave like a young dog, or whelp, unable to refrain from showing his happiness at the sight of his master. Like a whelp he is liable to indulge in many frolics and capers but not all of them are fruitless. He expands his theory of the "quarter-educated" and his idea of a journal called *Chit-chat*, much to Milvain's mirth and disbelief. Yet his venture is successful, and "that ass Whelpdale" finally becomes Milvain's brother-in-law by marrying his sister Dora.

Also he sets up a school to teach people how to write when he himself has failed as an artist, which leads Jasper to comment: "Now that's one of the finest jokes I ever heard. A man who can't get anyone to publish his own books makes a living by telling other people how to write." Yet the adage comes true which says "He laughs well who laughs last", because Whelpdale eventually becomes an important literary figure with his paper. "I believe it is a stroke of genius. *Chat* doesn't attract anyone, but *Chit-chat* would sell like hot-cakes, as they say in America. I know I am right, laugh as you will", says Whelpdale to Milvain.

Yule's Christian name Alfred cannot but remind us of the famous king Alfred the Great. There is nothing great about Alfred Yule and here again we feel the irony in the choice of the name. Alfred Yule has never succeeded in achieving any fame whatsoever and his work consists mainly in writing critical articles anonymously. Besides he has married a lower-class woman whom he has come to dislike because of her ignorance and Cockney-tainted speech. He clings to his last hope to attain literary fame (wreaking revenge on his adversaries at the same time) thanks to his daughter's inheritance, but this last opportunity is denied him and he becomes blind in the end. His surname Yule—an archaic word—suggests pedantry. Alfred Yule is pedantic and only relishes in book-learning and literary rivalry with men like Clement Fadge. Yule is a fount of erudite knowledge but a fount whose water has dried up with the years. A eulogistic footnote on his merits is one of the few joys of his life as P.J. Keating remarked in his study of *New Grub Street*.[3] Let us notice that the man with whom Yule quarrels bears a rather peaceful Christian name: Clement. As for the word *Fadge* or fudge (fadge being rather obsolete), it recalls a notion of

208

something made up in a dishonest way and this alludes undoubtedly to the literary quarrels and practices of the time.

Mrs. Goby, one of the minor characters, incarnates what Alfred Yule hates: illiteracy of the lower classes. Gissing transcribed their coarse speech phonetically to lay emphasis on their inferiority and ignorance ("I am Mrs. Goby, of the 'Olloway Road, wife of Mr. C.O. Goby, 'aberdasher"). Now in vulgar language a gob is a mouth and also a spittle, so here the character's name bears with it unpleasant connotations linked with the mouth. (Mrs. Goby cannot express herself properly and Alfred Yule quarrels with her for all that she represents.) The resemblance between Goby and gob is surely not mere coincidence, suggestive as it is.

Baker, another minor character in *New Grub Street*, tells about his difficulty with "compersition". He wants to raise himself and takes lessons with Biffen, yet he finds it hard to spell baker, as the saying is. Gissing seems to mock Baker's attempt to improve himself though the latter is making a praiseworthy effort to sit for an examination so as to be promoted.

To my mind the close examination of names and the meanings they carry with them bring evidence that Gissing was perfectly aware of the device which consists in carefully choosing names which evoke certain qualities or defects. We may feel sure that he made use of this device even if he did so more sparingly than Dickens, whom he admired. A scholar, having already perceived this trend to select "meaningful" names, has studied the subject on a large scale in Gissing's works as a whole.[4] Names have always exerted a fascination on both writers and readers, to such an extent that some of them have come to be used as common denominations. Can we always explain why we have remembered this or that name from a novel or a play? Why do they still resound in our ears? There seems to lie the task of the etymologist who must have recourse to the psycho-analyst— maybe—to account for their deeply-felt power, all the more so as interpretation varies from one reader to another.

Nevertheless we may say that this method contributes to some type of consistency in the drawing of characters as that alluded to by C.J. Francis in his article on heredity and environment: "Not for him [Gissing] are striking changes in character, radical conversions to good or evil such as may be found in romantic novels of the more facile kind. A slow development and alteration of attitudes can be seen in some characters, but it indicates no basic change." We may safely infer that the careful selection or creation of names is directly linked with the delineation of characters, their psychological relationships with other characters, their role, the way in which they react when confronted with specific problems, and to put it briefly with their doom in a novel: be it either success or failure.

Was not Gissing a lover of Greek and Latin authors, is it not justified to think that he kept in mind the notion of *fatum*—the very keystone of Greek tragedy—when writing his novels?

A tendency of Gissing's was morbidity: let us recall the indigent surgeon in *New Grub Street*: "I was christened Victor—possibly because I was doomed to defeat in life." The quotation speaks for itself and we are left little doubt as to Gissing's state of mind. Yet in spite of that, characters are not flat or deprived of any interest, they are not neatly depicted from the start or recognisable at first sight as the incarnations of symbols; for Gissing was perfectly aware of the complexity of human nature. Of Woodstock in *The Unclassed* he says: "Human nature is compact of strangely conflicting elements, and I have met men extremely brutal in one way yet were capable of a good deal of genial feeling in other directions".[5]

Complexity of character does not forcibly entail that they are apt to change radically towards the end of the novel or that a *coup de théâtre* is to be expected every now and then.

So it seems that the notion of fate forces itself upon the reader as he reaches the end of the novels and that men like Reardon have their own essence and cannot witness a complete change. The naming of characters seems to indicate and to further strengthen this impression, and in some way to materialize the abstract notions, the ideas which come to mind in the evocation of Gissing's characters.

210

NOTES

1. B. Bergonzi, "The novelist as hero", *Twentieth Century*, November 1958, pp. 444-55.
2. Q.D. Leavis, "Gissing and the English novel", *Scrutiny*, VII, June 1938, pp. 73-81.
3. *New Grub Street*, Studies in English Literature, No. 33 (Edward Arnold, 1968).
4. P.F. Kropholler, "On the Names of Gissing's Characters", *The Gissing Newsletter*, pp. 5-7.
5. Letter to his brother, 23 June 1884, *Letters of George Gissing to Members of his Family* (London, 1927), p. 141.

Index

213